Musical Theatre Auditions and Casting

A performer's guide viewed from both sides of the audition table

Neil Rutherford

With a Foreword by Bartlett Sher

methuen | drama

Published by Methuen Drama 2012

Methuen Drama, an imprint of Bloomsbury Publishing Plc

1 3 5 7 9 10 8 6 4 2

Methuen Drama
Bloomsbury Publishing Plc
50 Bedford Square
London WC1B 3DP
www.methuendrama.com

Copyright © Neil Rutherford 2012

Neil Rutherford has asserted his rights under the Copyright, Designs
and Patents Act, 1988, to be identified as the author of this work.
The photograph on p. 31 copyright © Chris Baker
(www.chrisbakerphotographer.com)

A CIP catalogue record for this book is available from the British Library

ISBN: 978 1 408 16062 6

Available in the USA from Bloomsbury Academic & Professional,
175 Fifth Avenue/3rd Floor, New York, NY 10010
www.BloomsburyAcademicUSA.com

Typeset by Helm Information, TN35 4SR www.helm-information.co.uk
Printed and bound in Great Britain by the MPG Books Group

CONTENTS

Section One: Before the Audition

Section Two: The Audition

Text work
Be brave
Asking questions
Looking at you in a new way
Readers
Accents
Dealing with poor text
Reading at sight
Dyslexia
Call-back songs
Keeping on top of your call-back
Group auditions
The final audition
The end of the audition process
The decision-making process
Profile casting
Approvals
Rejection
Feedback
Words of Wisdom

ACKNOWLEDGEMENTS

I would sincerely like to thank the following people, without whom this book would not have been written.

Anna Brewer and the team at Methuen Drama and Bloomsbury Publishing for their support, encouragement and trust in me.

All my colleagues at Ambassador Theatre Group, particularly Stuart Burt for being my partner in crime, for his friendship and for putting up with me, and Howard Panter for giving me the opportunities to learn my craft and work with such inspiring and talented people.

The contributors: Bill Deamer, Richard Eyre, Christopher Gattelli, David Gilmore, Jamie Lloyd, Christopher Luscombe, Joey McKneeley, Stephen Mear, Jerry Mitchell, Vanessa Scammell, Dominic Shaw, Bartlett Sher, David Taylor, Gareth Valentine; they are all masters at what they do and I have had the great good fortune to have worked with all of them. Despite their being so busy, I'm flattered that they have found a moment to write down their wise thoughts for this book.

Special thanks to Natalie Bush, Rhiannon Chesterman, David Gale, Dom Hodson, Lydia Jenkins, Christopher Leveaux, Oliver Savile, Alex Turney, Sam Wier and Alex Young for reading a final draft and giving me their valuable feedback. They are all recent graduates of Guildford School of Acting, Arts Educational School, Mountview Academy of Theatre Arts and the Royal Academy of Music and I wish them well in their future careers. And to my pals Wayne Fitzsimmons and fellow casting director Duncan Stewart for their input on several sections throughout the book.

To Graham Taylor for encouraging me in the initial concept of this book.

To Dom, Big Josh and Adey for always being there.

To my family, Keryle, Iain and Carl, for their love and support, and particularly my nephew Josh who constantly reminds me that it's vital never to neglect the child within us, no matter how old we may be.

And finally a massive thanks to all those I've auditioned for, auditioned with or who have auditioned for me over the years, every one of whom has contributed in some small way to this book.

FOREWORD

Auditioning is an art unto itself, and worth separating from the art of acting for a play or musical. People who love auditioning have the qualities of athletes who love to practise, of people who see their work as something to be applied in any circumstance, and of people who value bravery and fearlessness in their approach to life.

Good auditionees do not measure the success of an audition by the validation of their work through employment or through praise. One must demonstrate enormous psychological health to enjoy auditioning and not place this activity in the realm of approval.

Take a scene or song, analyse it, enjoy it, and bend your craft towards it. Go into the room to explore the words and the part, ask yourself hard questions about the action of the scene or the song, put that action into the character and particularly the person the scene is aimed at, keep the focus off yourself and on the work, and be brave and agile. Make clear choices and look at the work like a separate application of acting, compressed into fragments of a part, and distil the work to an essence. Make bold choices, and clear choices, with an ability to repeat. Value language, speech, the sound and potential of the human voice, and be aware of the subtle information the human body can impart through shape and gesture.

When the audition is over, let it go and move on. Try not to live in the matrix of hope and guessing and a demeaning sense of longing. A great auditionee once told me, 'I always imagine that when I'm done, I spit on the floor and leave.' Nobody is interested in somebody who wants something too desperately. They are interested in someone who is good.

Always expect the person holding the audition to treat you with respect and care. Think the best of the person putting you through this, whether casting director or director. Always remember, no matter how something goes, that the people holding the audition actually want you to be right, and to be great.

And finally, if you are lucky, you will be walking into a room with Neil Rutherford, a person who knows this complex art better than anybody. And a person who loves actors with all his heart and who understands what it takes to make of an audition something like painting a beautiful miniature. And certainly Neil knows more, for he knows the profound art that is to be found in an audition.

Bartlett Sher
Director

CONTRIBUTORS' BIOGRAPHIES

Bill Deamer is an international and West End choreographer. His work includes the world premiere of *Top Hat* (Aldwych Theatre); new choreography on *Love Never Dies* (Adelphi Theatre); *Evita*, European and national tour; *Jekyll and Hyde*, European and national tour; *The Boyfriend*, Regents Park Open Air Theatre, Olivier Award – choreographer. *Babes In Arms* (Chichester Festival Theatre); *Barbara Cook in Concert* (London Coliseum); *Follies in Concert* (London Palladium); *Lady be Good* (Regents Park Open Air Theatre); *Side by Side in Concert* (Novello Theatre). Television includes choreography on *So You Think You Can Dance* (BBC) and *Strictly Come Dancing* (BBC).

Richard Eyre was Director of the National Theatre 1988–97, where his productions included *Guys and Dolls, The Beggar's Opera, Hamlet, Racing Demon, Richard III, Night of the Iguana, Skylight, La Grande Magia, John Gabriel Borkman, Amy's View, King Lear* and *The Invention of Love*. Since then his work includes *Mary Poppins, Betty Blue Eyes, Vincent in Brixton, The Crucible, Private Lives, La Traviata, The Marriage of Figaro* and *Carmen*. His films include *Iris* and *Notes on a Scandal*. He has published four books. He has received many theatre, film and TV awards and was knighted in 1997.

Christopher Gattelli is an award-winning director, choreographer and musical stager. His work includes *South Pacific* at the Lincoln Center (Tony and Outer Critics Circle nominations), London and Australia. On Broadway: *Newsies; Godspell; Sunday in the Park with George; 13: The Musical; The Ritz; Martin Short: Fame Becomes Me; High Fidelity.* In the West End/London: *Silence! The Musical; Sunday in the Park With George; Tick, Tick … Boom!* Off-Broadway: *Altar Boyz* (Lortel, Callaway Awards, Drama Desk nomination); *Bat Boy: The Musical* (Lortel Award); *Tick, Tick … Boom!; 10 Million Miles; Adrift in Macao; I Love You Because.*

David Gilmore's musical work as a director includes *Lend Me a Tenor* at the Globe, and the award-winning musical *The Hired Man* by Melvyn Bragg and Howard Goodall, both produced by Andrew Lloyd Webber. His production of *Grease* ran for seven years at the Dominion and Cambridge Theatres before returning to the Victoria Palace and recently the Piccadilly. It has also played in many European and Asian cities since. He has worked frequently in Australia, where he recently directed the musical *Footloose* in Sydney as well as Andrew Lloyd Webber's *Song and Dance* in Sydney, Melbourne and Adelaide. Other West End productions include *Annie Get Your Gun* and the Cole Porter revue *A Swell Party* at the Vaudeville.

Jamie Lloyd is a British theatre director, and an Associate Director of the Donmar Warehouse, where he recently directed *The 25th Annual Putnam County Spelling Bee, Passion* (winning the *Evening Standard* Award for Best Musical) and *Piaf,* transferring to the West End. His other West End credits include *Three Days of Rain, The Little Dog Laughed,* and Pinter's *The Lover* and *The Collection.* He directed *The Pride* at the Royal Court, for which he won the Olivier Award for Outstanding Achievement in an Affiliate Theatre, and *She*

Stoops to Conquer at the Royal National Theatre. He recently directed *Inadmissible Evidence* at the Donmar, and Alexi Kaye Campbell's new play *The Faith Machine* at the Royal Court.

Christopher Luscombe's UK directing credits include *The Shakespeare Revue* (Vaudeville), *Star Quality* (Apollo), *Home and Beauty* (Lyric), *Fascinating Aïda – One Last Flutter* (Olivier Award nomination for Best Entertainment, Comedy Theatre), *The Rocky Horror Show* (Playhouse), *The Comedy of Errors* and *The Merry Wives of Windsor* (Shakespeare's Globe), *Enjoy* (Gielgud), *When We Are Married* (Olivier Award nomination for Best Revival, Garrick), *The Madness of George III* (Apollo), *Masterpieces* (Birmingham Rep), *Little Shop of Horrors* and *The History Boys* (West Yorkshire Playhouse), *The Likes of Us* (Sydmonton), and tours of *The Importance of Being Earnest, Tell Me on a Sunday, The Lady in the Van, Lord Arthur Savile's Crime, Single Spies* and *Spamalot.*

Joey McKneely has directed and choreographed *West Side Story* throughout the world including a sold-out run in London (Olivier nomination/Best Musical Revival). He was also the Reproduction Choreographer for the new Broadway revival of *West Side Story* directed by Arthur Laurents. On Broadway, Joey's choreographic debut was *Smokey Joe's Cafe,* followed by *The Life, Twelfth Night* (Lincoln Center), *The Wild Party,* and *The Boy from Oz.* He has earned two Tony Award nominations, two Outer Critics Circle nominations, an NAACP Image Award, and an LA Ovation Award. He has also directed/choreographed US national tours of *Thoroughly Modern Millie, Annie Get Your Gun, Crazy for You,* and the off-Broadway production of Jerry Herman's revue, *Showtune.* In addition, he has directed Andrew Lloyd Webber and Ben Elton's *The Beautiful Game* in Japan.

Stephen Mear's London choreographic credits include *Crazy For You*; *Betty Blue Eyes*; *Shoes* Director and Choreographer (What's on Stage nomination); *Sweet Charity* (Olivier nomination); *Hello, Dolly!* (Olivier for Best Choreography); *Gigi*; *Mary Poppins* (joint choreographer with Matthew Bourne, Olivier for Best Choreography, Tony and Drama Desk nomination for Best Choreography, LA Drama Circle Critics Award for Best Choreography and the Helpmann Award for Best Choreography); *Sinatra* (Olivier nomination); *On The Town*; *Acorn Antiques*; *Tonight's the Night, Anything Goes* (Olivier for Outstanding Musical Production); *Singing in the Rain* (Olivier nomination for Best Choreography); *Soul Train* (Olivier nomination for Best Choreography); *The Little Mermaid* (Broadway). In 2009 Stephen also became Associate Director/Choreographer at Chichester Festival Theatre where, among many projects, he has recently directed and choreographed *She Loves Me*.

Jerry Mitchell made his directorial debut with *Legally Blonde* (Broadway, London and Australia), winning Tony, Olivier and Drama Desk Awards. Jerry received a Tony Award as choreographer of the 2005 revival of *La Cage aux Folles*, also being nominated for *Dirty Rotten Scoundrels*. He received Olivier and Tony nominations for choreographing *Hairspray* and *The Full Monty*. For Broadway, he choreographed *Never Gonna Dance*, *Gypsy*, *The Rocky Horror Show* and *You're a Good Man, Charlie Brown*, and *Hedwig and the Angry Inch* (Off-Broadway and film). Recent projects include *Peepshow* in Las Vegas, and work on musicals *Kinky Boots*, *Mad Hot Ballroom* and *Queen of the Stardust Ballroom*, which he will direct and choreograph for Broadway.

Vanessa Scammell's recent Music Director/Conductor credits include: *South Pacific* Australian tour; *West Side Story*

Australian tour, *Chicago* Australasian tour; *The Phantom of the Opera* Australian and Asian tour; *Damn Yankees* – The Production Company; *The Helpmann Awards* (2008–11); *Fiddler on the Roof* – Sydney; *Titanic* – Seabiscuit Productions; *Cats* world tour; and *Into the Woods*. Opera Australia engagements include *South Pacific, La Traviata,* and orchestral credits include the *Adelaide Cabaret Festival and Orchestra Victoria in Concert*. Vanessa was the joint winner of the Brian Stacey Award for emerging Australian conductors in 2008 and completed a Masters of Music in Conducting at the Sydney Conservatorium of Music in 2011.

Dominic Shaw is the Associate Director/Choreographer for the *Legally Blonde* UK tour and was Resident Director/Choreographer on *Legally Blonde* in the West End. His theatre work includes *Aïda;* Gus and Bobby C in *Saturday Night Fever* – Dusseldorf; Dance Captain/Swing and understudy Link Larkin and Corny Collins in the original London cast of *Hairspray* – and original London cast of *Wicked*; *Top of the Pops* – BBC; *Love on a Saturday Night* – Granada and *The Royal Variety Performance* (2006 and 2007). His choreography work includes *Tonight's the Night* – BBC; *Comic Relief* – BBC and *This Morning* and *West End Live* with *Hairspray*. Dominic is also a songwriter and has written and produced an album called *Remedy,* which is available on iTunes.

Bartlett Sher is Resident Director at the Lincoln Center, having directed *Joe Turner's Come and Gone* (Tony nomination), *Women on the Verge of a Nervous Breakdown, South Pacific* (Tony, Drama Desk and Outer Critics Circle Awards), *Awake and Sing!* (Tony nomination), and *The Light in the Piazza* (Tony nomination). He was Artistic Director of Seattle's Intiman Theatre (2000–10), credits there including the world premieres of *Prayer for My Enemy* and *Singing Forest* by

Craig Lucas (both also Long Wharf Theatre) and *Nickel and Dimed*; plays by Chekhov, Wilder, Shakespeare, Goldoni and Tony Kushner. Opera includes *The Barber of Seville* and *The Tales of Hoffmann* (Metropolitan Opera), *Roméo et Juliette* (Salzburg Festival), *Mourning Becomes Electra* (Seattle Opera and New York City Opera) and *Two Boys* (ENO). New York work also includes *Prayer for My Enemy* (Playwrights); *Cymbeline* (2001 Callaway Award for Best Director), *Waste* (2000 Best Play Obie), *Don Juan* (all TFANA).

David Taylor, award-winning American director, originally consulted at Sundance Theatre Festival before directing *Queen of the Stardust Ballroom* in Chicago. David supervised the transfer from Broadway of *A Chorus Line* to Drury Lane followed by his London debut, *They're Playing Our Song*. He directed *Dear Anyone, Pump Boys and Dinettes* and *Can-Can* – all in the West End – followed by a new version of *Chess* in New York, and a spectacular production of *The Wizard of Oz* in Toronto. David directed Andrew Lloyd Webber's *Cats* in Toronto and Germany, and it had long and successful runs in each continent. Recent projects include *Monkee Business*.

Gareth Valentine, Musical Supervisor, was musical supervisor/dance arranger/musical director for *Anything Goes* at Drury Lane and the Royal National Theatre. A long list of West End theatre credits includes *My One and Only, Kiss Me, Kate, Merrily We Roll Along, Chicago, Damn Yankees, Nine, Camelot, Company, Kiss of the Spider Woman, Miss Saigon, The Baker's Wife, Cats, Cabaret, Toad of Toad Hall, 42nd Street, Acorn Antiques, Porgy and Bess, Wicked, The King and I, Into The Woods, Crazy For You* and *Strictly Gershwin*. As a composer, his *Requiem*, recorded at Abbey Road Studios, London, and performed in London, Australia, Scandinavia and the States, has met with international acclaim.

INTRODUCTION

Since the age of ten, you've dreamed of being in a musical, even if it means singing at the back while your musical theatre heroine takes centre stage and flies above you, either defying gravity, riding in an old car with wings or allowing the winds of change to whisk her, and her parrot-headed umbrella, to another bunch of annoying Edwardian brats. You might have been in the profession for several years, spending significantly more time working in call centres than in the rehearsal room. Or maybe you've just left drama college where, for the last few years, you enjoyed making a complete fool of yourself regularly forgetting the words of *Another Thousand People Just Got Off of the Plane* or debating whether a particular musical really is the greatest ever written. Your final-year showcase was fun: two minutes and twenty seconds in front of stony-faced, humourless, perplexed agents and casting directors. At least you got a few business cards afterwards from agents who specialise in 'exotic dancing'.

But it's all going to be OK; you still sing fairly well (despite having changed your vocal range on your CV from soprano to bass due to too many late nights), you dance spectacularly (at weddings) and you can act well enough; of course, you have to be a fairly good actor in order to make those anonymous calls at your 'day job', where you spend eight hours a day selling 'charity' balloons for a balloon race that your boss has secretly told you will never take place.

And then, just as you ponder whether you have more chance of getting into the new Rob Flosse musical, *Illinois*, by applying for the *Z Factor*, your mobile rings to the melody of 'I Feel Witty'.

'Hello?'

'Darling, it's Dorothy.' Silence. Dorothy?

'I'm sorry. Dorothy who?'

'Dorothy! From Oz!' Still nothing. Then, in hushed tones, 'Your agent?'

Ah yes – the memory of that scintillating tar-soaked voice stirs. Those theatrical tones, the drama and excitement, the sense of purpose and fulfilment.

'Oh, hi Dorothy! Sorry, miles away.'

'Well, I hope not too far, darling. We've got you an audition, dear. This afternoon. I did leave several messages on your phone …'

You sweat. An audition? Surely not! You've only had two auditions in the last six months, including the advert where you had to be a cat on heat for an avant-garde chocolate bar commercial for Europe.

'Oh, that's great, Deirdre … um, Dorothy.'

'Do you have a pen and paper handy?' You don't, no. 'It's this afternoon. Someone's dropped out of *Hamelot* and they need a walking understudy urgently'.

'Understudy?!? WALKING UN-DER-STU-DY!!!'

'Well, darling, you can't be too choosy in this climate. It'll be good for you. Your West End debut! So, four-twenty at Banana Dance Studios; you're the last one in. Take some jazz shoes. You'll sing first, but they may ask you to dance.'

'OK – thanks, Davina. Speak later.'

You hang up in a panic. Three hours to go. It takes fifty minutes to get home in order to pick up your dance shoes and find some music. And that's not including the argument time it takes to persuade your balloon boss to let you leave for the rest of the day.

You dive in your front door and by the time you're up the stairs, you already know that you'll wear those red cut-off, ripped jeans and the emerald-green 'I Love Idina' T-shirt you got off the internet. But where are your jazz shoes? Close to Narnia the last time you looked at the back of the wardrobe. Oh, never mind about the shoes. Your gold trainers will be fine, and didn't you read somewhere online that there wasn't much dancing in this production anyway?

You grab a handful of songs, dab some product in your hair and you're out the door again, with just enough time to purchase a new deodorant spray from the corner shop on the way to the station. On the platform, you have a look at the opening bars of your songs without pulling them from their plastic covers – 'I Want to Break Three' (your rock number) and 'Kiss Away The Sky' (your ballad). Both favourites and contrasting well with each other just as you'd been taught. Of course, you meant to have 'I Want To Break Three' transcribed down a bit, now that your voice has dropped several octaves. But it's OK, the pianist will be able to transpose it at sight, won't he? Having looked at the opening bars of each song, you put them next to your bag, and sit calmly with eyes closed, beginning your audition meditation.

After getting off at the wrong station (because you forgot to check the address of the studio) and having run to the correct address, you arrive at four-thirty-six. Phew just made it for the four-forty audition. You head up the stairs to Studio 2, where *Hamelot* is auditioning.

At the top of the stairs, an impressively coiffed chap stands with a clipboard. You saunter up coolly.

'Kerrington.' You mumble your surname in his direction.

'Sorry?'

'K-E-R-R-I-N-G-T-O-N. Four-forty p.m. Dorothy Palmer Associates.'

'Oh. You're late. Another minute and they'd have packed up and gone. You were supposed to be here at four-twenty.'

'I was told four-forty.' You give him a sharp look.

'Well, Dorothy was specifically told four-twenty. I set it up myself and explained you were the last one so not to be late.'

'Well, it's not my fault. Just let me in if they're all waiting.'

'They're running over at the moment and someone's already in there. Why don't you sit down for a second, and take the weight off your tongue.'

And rather put out, he flounces into the audition room, closing the door abruptly behind him.

You then begin to hear the tones of the most superb vocal you've ever heard.

'Kiss Away The Sky …' gently floats under the door as your mouth begins to dry. 'The sweetness of tomorrow …' 'That's my song!' you think. 'My special song.' 'We know what we've all been through …' And now you'll have to do 'I Want to Break Three', and without a warm-up too. Having forgotten to buy some water, you start to cough a few times, hoping the locked phlegm will loosen itself. The amazing voice is getting to the climax of the song and with the old adage 'If you can't beat 'em …', you join in in an attempt to warm up your voice. Louder and louder until you suddenly realise that the voice from the other side of the door has stopped, and you've probably shrieked several painful notes by yourself and easily within earshot of the audition panel inside.

You begin to perspire a little more, and are glad of the deodorant you bought. Two sprays underarm do the trick, except that you also inhaled some of the vapour, which adds further unease to your vocal cords.

The door opens just as you start a coughing fit, and out pops

Clipboard Boy and your arch-enemy, Angel, from college.

'Darling! How are you?'

'Hi, Dale. Great, thanks.'

'How's things? Saw your cameo last week on the TV. Lovely. You were … great. What you up to?'

'Just finishing at the Savoy; you know, *Roundabout*, the job I got out of college.'

'Oh yeah. I heard it was a bit crap. Haven't seen it of course – didn't think I should waste my money. Sorry.' Clipboard Boy gives a stare.

'Ready?' you ask him petulantly, and with a reference towards Clipboard Boy, you whisper to Angel (but still to be heard), 'ASMs!' and air-kiss a goodbye.

Clipboard Boy opens the door to the room and announces you dispassionately. You walk in, with a confidence that only someone with red cut-off jeans can, towards the centre of the room.

Silence. Stillness.

More silence. More stillness.

Just as you think you've stepped into a Pinter scene, you decide to cough in order to get the audition panel's attention. Of the seven people behind the desk, an odd-looking figure wearing way too much pink looks up.

'Ah … Kerrington? Dale Kerrington? Don't look much like your photo. Greetings. I'm Lou, the director. This is …' and a host of meaningless people nod and grimace as they are introduced. Finally Lou references Clipboard Boy, who you've just noticed is now sitting on the end of the row. '… and Jason, my associate director, who's just directed the new hit *Roundabout* at the Savoy. You may have seen it …'

Jason's wry smile says it all.

'I'd like to sing 'Kiss Away The Sky'.

'Mmmm …' says Lou, followed by murmurings of disapproval at the table. 'Do you have anything else?'

'I Want To Break Three' from *We Will Shock You*?'

'Nothing else? This is *Hamelot,* after all; I'd have expected something from the Golden Era at least.'

You shake your head, having no idea what that is. 'Well, if that's all you've got …'

You walk over to the piano and plonk down your music. The pianist takes the sheets out of the plastic wallets, and finds single, damaged, untaped pages with no page numbers. The lyrics are all worn, or covered in pencil markings, so it's difficult to tell which page comes first. You take a minute to rearrange your music, hearing further grumps from the panel behind you. In order to help the accompanist, you thump out a beat with your fist on top of the piano, rather faster than you would have liked since you're a little nervous, and begin to walk back to the centre.

Before you've composed yourself, the pianist plays three bars of chords – nothing like what you remember from the cast album – and stops.

You look at him; he looks at you. A hay bale sweeps across the room as you go for your pistols.

'Oh, sorry. I forgot to say, can you take it down into A flat, please?' You clap your hands to the beat, with an accompanying stomp on the floor, and the pianist starts over, lower this time. You watch him intently for your moment to come in, and he generously gives you a nod. Hurray – you're off! You started in the right place, but the key is completely wrong. Although the pianist has lowered the key into A flat, you've somehow managed to start an octave higher and you now resemble the sound of a chipmunk on helium. After what seems like an eternity, although it was in fact only nineteen bars, the hand of Lou waves, stopping the pianist.

'Sorry to stop you, darling. It's fascinating, really, absolutely fascinating. But truthfully, love, I'm not entirely sure you're ready for the professional theatre, dear.'

You nod sheepishly as you leave for the door, forgetting your music at the piano and overhearing Clipboard Boy's final comment: 'Nor ready for auditions, frankly ...'

————

Of course, an extreme audition story like this would never happen in real life and I'm sure you picked out the forty or so errors that Kerrington made in this brief little tale. But a large proportion of the actors I meet (and throughout the book I'll refer to both male and female performers as actors) find auditioning very difficult, whether they have recently left musical theatre training or have been in the business for years. In an overcrowded market, anything you can do to help improve your success rate in gaining those important credits on your CV must surely be of benefit, and I'm therefore delighted you have chosen this book.

Of course, if you found the imaginary tale above has struck a particular dis-chord, then this book is definitely for you. Some people audition well, others find it an excruciating experience. During the years I've spent as a casting director, I've seen many wonderful performers fall at the very first hurdle simply because they don't audition well. Even seasoned professionals make basic audition mistakes, not dissimilar (in part) to the fictitious character of our story.

Indeed many recent musical theatre graduates I speak to feel that they are not often prepared for the professional audition room, despite excellent training. In common with other casting director colleagues I find visiting drama schools, as well as taking master classes, a hugely enjoyable and satisfying part of my job. We hope that when actors meet us in the 'real' world, it won't be quite so daunting. But those classroom sessions are often limited and only reach out to a comparatively small number of people.

I have therefore set out to write a casting and audition technique book which will help students, graduates, professionals and anyone auditioning for a musical to overcome some of the obstacles and encourage them to audition confidently and give them the best opportunity to land the jobs that excite them. Unless you're fortunately positioned to get offers of work without having to audition, then auditioning is going to be vitally important to you. Indeed, you're certainly going to be auditioning many more times than you're going to be signing contracts.

As a professional actor for many years, I attended numerous auditions which resulted in me being a successful 'jobbing' actor, working predominantly in London's West End musicals. As a result, I know *exactly* what it's like to stand up in front of a multitude of people staring at me from behind a huge table and deciding upon my fate.

Since becoming a casting director, I've gained extensive knowledge of the casting process, having cast professional musicals and plays both in my role as an independent casting director and as the Head of Casting at the Ambassador Theatre Group, one of the UK's leading theatre producers and theatre owners.

Having sat on both sides of the audition table at the very highest levels gives me a unique perspective on the audition process. I hope that all I've observed from this perspective provides beneficial insight and advice for you throughout this book. Even if one piece of advice means you land that next role, then it will have been a worthwhile experience for both of us. Depending on your level of training, some of this book may tell you what you already know. If so, then I hope it provides a refresher course for you, with all the information you've been taught in one place.

A few honest words up front. What I can't do is provide you with the raw talent; I'm a great believer that talent is a natural gift bestowed upon you, which you can then nurture and improve through training as well as the experience gained from working within the business itself. And talent, at the end of the day, is what is going to get you the jobs. What I do aim to do in this book, however, is to provide some ideas and give some guidance, which will, I hope, allow your talent to shine, enabling you to remain confident throughout the audition process.

Views do differ, of course, and the information I provide is taken from my own personal experience. There will certainly be different schools of thought and when I know of opposing views, I will endeavour to point them out, and advise which you should choose for specific situations. Every audition process, and every audition panel, will be a unique challenge and you must therefore use your intelligence to decipher which of the points raised within the book are right for each situation. But the tools and ideas here do work and with diligence and experience you'll soon get to know which work best for each situation and for you. To help pinpoint some ideas, throughout the book you will find 'Key Thoughts' in boxes, and also many questions that I get asked frequently, which are in bold italics. At the end of each chapter, there are tips and advice from some of the world's leading directors, choreographers and musical directors relating to the relevant chapter sections, headed 'Words of Wisdom'.

Finally, results don't just fall in your lap. Just reading this book is not going to make a jot of difference if you don't work hard and put everything into practice. So much about the success of your audition is about the work you do even before getting into the audition room.

I hope you will find this book enjoyable and insightful, entertaining and practical, and most of all, a companion and guide that will be useful for the rest of your auditioning life. Our business is one of the most rewarding and fulfilling occupations; my greatest wish is that these pages will help you to achieve your own goals in making your future years as a musical theatre performer even more gratifying and rewarding.

SECTION ONE

BEFORE THE AUDITION

1

HOW THE AUDITION PROCESS WORKS

The phone rings.

'Darling, it's Dorothy.'

'Hi, Dorothy ...' You pull the bed covers a little closer.

'You sound groggy, dear. Late night?'

'Didn't get in till three a.m. Had to clean all the tables, set up for the breakfast shift, empty the dishwashers ...'

'Well, Cinders, you're going to the ball. I've got a spare ticket to the opening of *Hamelot* tonight. Come with me – there's a casting director I want to introduce you to. And while we're there, we can discuss those wonderful new headshots you've had done ...'

You may well ask yourself, '*Why do I need to know about the audition process? I just want to get into the audition room, sing, act, dance and get the job.*' I can understand that. In terms of you – the performer – you'll get cast on your performances in the room on the day of your initial audition and subsequent call-backs (also called 'recalls' – I'm going to use the term call-backs throughout the book). Who cares about the process before your audition?

Yet I hear so many actors complain that they weren't seen for such and such a musical or that a certain casting director dislikes them. Surely, then, it's useful for you to know about the work that gets done before you get into the room, because it may help you to understand how much thought goes into our preparation for the production and the process we go through in order to find you. Most importantly, if you understand the odds you're up against, it will also help you in terms of your own preparation within the business, and what you've already achieved before you've danced a step, sung a note or read a line.

Who are casting directors and what do they do?

Shortly after I became a casting director, a well-known and successful director grabbed my arm at a press night party, spilling a glass of red wine over one of my favourite jackets. After the initial kerfuffle of trying to blot the wine off my jacket, he proceeded to interrogate me.

'And what are you doing, dear?' he blurted. 'Haven't seen you on stage recently ... resting?'

'I've given myself over to the Dark Side,' I said proudly, mopping myself down with a napkin. 'I'm Head of Casting for the Ambassador Theatre Group.'

'Oh no!' He gasped theatrically, a look of disgust spreading over his face. 'A casting director! Scum of the earth, dear, scum of the earth! A pointless job – any director worth their salt knows which actors they want in their company.'

Slightly taken aback, I gave him my business card and we promised ourselves a supper to catch up on old times. The meal never transpired. But the irony was that this same director called me up regularly for years afterwards asking for additional ideas of actors for specific roles he was trying to cast.

'I don't need a casting director of course, darling, but it would be wonderful to have your input.' I bit my lip.

Some directors are very good at knowing and remembering actors, and certainly have favourites with whom they regularly work. And some directors or producers don't use a casting director at all, preferring to use actors they've worked with in the past, seen in performance or know by other means.

But the fact is that not every director can possibly know every actor. At the time of writing, there are currently almost 36,500 actors registered as full members with British Actors Equity (and a further 5,000 students with provisional memberships), just over 48,000 members with American Equity, 40,000 registered on Spotlight (the UK's leading online casting database) and 15,000 actors on Showcast in Australia. It's obviously impossible for a casting director to know each and every one of these actors in their respective countries, but given that a key responsibility of a casting director is to suggest actors to producers, directors and other members of the creative team, we probably have a wider knowledge base than most and are arguably more proactive in regularly seeing actors in productions, workshops, classes and understudy runs and discovering students in their final-year productions and graduate showcases.

And so the role of a casting director has become important within the creative process for most professional productions. Indeed, casting the right actors, whether in leading roles or not, can make a significant impact on the success or failure of a production.

In a nutshell, I see my role as a casting director as having several key functions:

- *Sourcing talent* – being able to present the creative team (director, choreographer, producer, musical director, etc.) with a range of actors who, following initial discussions, it's felt may be appropriate for the role in question.

- *Setting up auditions* – a casting director and his/her office will normally set up your audition time as well as send out audition material (scripts and music), give you feedback and notes on characterisation, and book audition rooms and pianists/readers. The exception is the Open Audition Call, which we'll deal with in Chapter 4.

• *Running the audition room* – most casting directors will 'run the room'; among other things they will look after the panel, take overall charge in welcoming the actor, leading the actor in discussion and guiding them through the audition, and closing the audition off. Some directors, or another member of the creative team, may wish to take some of these responsibilities. Others prefer to sit back and observe. It will change depending on the personality of the team.

• *Mediating the casting process* – creative people are often outspoken (it tends to come with the territory of being passionately artistic) and while everyone on the audition panel has the common goal of desiring the very best and most wonderfully talented cast available to us, there can often be debate about which actors should be considered. I believe it's the responsibility of a casting director to mediate these sometimes difficult discussions, by keeping an overview of the casting process and who's been seen, and by using the knowledge base of a particular actor's abilities to feed into the discussion. If, for example, I know that someone – for whatever reason – has not lived up to their potential in the audition room, then it's my job as casting director to speak up for them and suggest to the auditioning panel that they might see them again and hope the actor will prove themselves better at a call-back. A casting director is therefore integral in bringing everyone's point of view together in order to aid the final decision of which actors to offer the roles to.

- *Reporting back on the audition/feedback* – most casting directors will aim to report back and give feedback to actors who have auditioned. This will be discussed later on in Chapter 5.

For some independent/freelance casting directors, that may be where their responsibility stops – presenting a high standard of actors appropriate to the role and being mediator in the post-audition discussions with the creative team. By the time the audition process is complete and the collective decision about who to cast is finalised, their job is effectively done and they wait in anticipation of the first performance.

With some producing companies, such as the Royal National Theatre, the Donmar Warehouse, the Royal Shakespeare Company and Ambassador Theatre Group in the UK, and the Lincoln Center, Roundabout Theatre Company, Playwrights Horizons, MTC, and the Public in America, the resident casting director may have additional responsibilities. These could include making offers and negotiating with agents or agent-less actors, developing an ongoing relationship with the actors once the rehearsal process begins and further throughout the run of the production, ironing out any cast issues along the way.

Generally, during the audition process, the casting office will be the first port of call rather than the producer. Some producers also have general managers, who may be responsible for negotiating actor deals after the casting has taken place and who will liaise with the casting office throughout the audition process.

Initial conversations

Having already discussed and agreed the production with the producer, the director (and possibly the choreographer and musical director if they've been engaged by that point) will discuss their ideas for each of the roles with the casting director. Everyone will have already read the script by this point, and I tend to go into those early meetings with a wide list of actors who I feel represent the character. If the piece is a new work, these first discussions with the director may be quite lengthy. But at the end of these discussions we will normally have decided upon:

- the age range for each role

- vocal range (defined by the vocal score, although keys are sometimes changed to suit the voice of the actor finally cast)

- the physicality of each role (in terms of weight, height and other elements of physical appearance)

- accent requirement

- character type

- sex of the role (not as daft as you might think … it's possible for a role to be played by the opposite sex. When producing Michael Grandage's acclaimed production of *Guys and Dolls* in Australia, Magda Szubanski played the male role of Big Jule. Similarly, Lea DeLaria played Eddie in *The Rocky Horror Show* in New York. There have been female Hamlets and all-male productions of Shakespeare. At the time of writing there are at least five roles in London's West End where our leading male actors spend a lot of time in a dress, not to mention a host of Cagelles and drag queens from *Priscilla, Queen of the Desert*).

Further discussions may refine these early decisions, or upon additional re-writes, readings or workshops of the musical these initial ideas may change completely. Even throughout the audition process it's not uncommon for the auditioning team to continue to redefine what they are looking for, or indeed for an actor to come in with qualities we love and may not have previously thought about, refining our thoughts further.

How do casting directors find actors?

Following on from these initial discussions between the producers, director and other members of the creative team, the casting director's next responsibility is to find the actors to present before the team.

There are a variety of ways in which we can achieve this, including:

- sending casting breakdowns to agents requesting actor suggestions

- using a personal or online casting database

- building casting lists based on our knowledge of actors

- seeing actors in work

- direct submissions from actors

- direct submissions from the creative team

- networking – meeting actors at social events or the theatre, etc.

- reputation – hearing about actors from others.

The casting breakdown

No, not the psychological breakdown I have when, having seen a hundred people in one long tiring day, no one has impressed us and we can't cast a single role. No, by casting breakdown I mean the device by which we relay to agents and artists what type of actors we are seeking for each role to be cast.

Breakdowns are generally sent to agents either by fax, email or via an online casting service such as SBS, PCR, the Spotlight Interactive (all UK), Showcast (Australia), or Breakdown Express, Actors Access (US). I will normally send a full breakdown to most agents. Do bear in mind however that not all the characters may be included on a breakdown as we might have cast certain roles already.

A typical breakdown for a specific role could read as follows (where the name of the musical, who's directing it, who's producing it and the dates of the production, audition dates and whether it tours, etc. will also be stated):

ROLE: JAY MICHAELS – MALE – 20s
Jay is a straight-talking, fun guy, wearing his heart on his sleeve. Enjoying his life, he's pleased to share his good luck with others and inspire them with his cheeky humour. This is a comic role requiring an actor with excellent comic timing and energy. Ideally handsome, with good physique. Jazz dance and great rock tenor voice with strong top G.

Needless to say, there is specific information contained within this breakdown which suggests whether you have the right qualities or not to be considered for the role.

Agents and submissions

A breakdown is sent out to agents and they will then submit their actors who most accurately represent what is required. Submissions are made either via an online casting service, by email or by hard copy to the casting director's office.

This brings us to a very important element of the whole audition process – and, of course, your entire career as an actor: your agent.

Your relationship with your agent

There are many words to be said about your relationship with your agent which don't really fall into the remit of a book on casting and auditioning. In a nutshell, trust and respect of each other, both personally and in terms of your responsibilities to each other, are vital. In terms of the audition process you need to ensure that your agent is fully aware of all your talents. You may only have had two minutes at your final graduation showcase to sing a song and had a short duologue thrust upon you. But how do they know what else you can do outside of that? In reality, they may also have seen you in your final-year college productions, so probably have a wider grasp of your talents than you were able to show at the showcase. Nevertheless, between the two of you, you must explore your talents to the full. A good agent will come to see you perform in your professional productions, or at least send their assistant if they have one. This isn't just about supporting you. It's about seeing a new side to your talents in order for them to build up a wider picture of your performance skills. And if you're lucky they'll bring a casting director too so we can all sing your praises.

As their responsibility is to keep tabs on your range of

skills in order to submit you for the right role, so it's your responsibility to tell them when you have new skills to add to your actor's file. It sounds such a simple thing but so many forget and as a result may not get the castings they are right for. A golden rule though, which you will note occurs several times throughout this book:

BE HONEST

**If you say you can do something,
you have to be able to do it;
be truthful to your agent, be truthful on your CV,
and be truthful at your audition.**

When we were casting the 2009 UK tour of *West Side Story*, the creative team had decided that the role of Tony had to sing the top B♭ in 'Maria' rather than the optional, lower top G. On the breakdown, we specifically asked for tenors who could effortlessly hit a top B♭. And reiterated the fact when we set up meetings with the actors. Despite this, tenor after tenor came in, cracking and fluffing the B♭, making the team more and more depressed and, effectively, wasting everyone's time. We have to assume that some of this was down to nerves, sore throats and just a 'bad day', all of which we'll discuss later. But the majority simply didn't have a B♭ in them.

This situation can be deeply frustrating. Between you and your agent, be sure that you fit the criteria of the breakdown. If a casting director's breakdown is too vague, then that's the casting director's fault. But if the breakdown is explicit, and you can't achieve what is required by the time the auditions are due to take place, that is the fault of you and your agent.

Do casting directors choose actors based on which agent represents them?

Casting directors will consider any actor an agent submits who accurately fits the breakdown for each role. And casting directors certainly value their relationships with agents. Inevitably there are people you want to do business with and people you don't; everyone has favourites but first and foremost we are seeking the most talented, appropriate actors, rather than doing favours for friends. Conversely, there are two agents I simply will not do business with because they've been so aggressively rude to me in the past. I know that sounds precious and I'm truly sorry that their actors miss out. Both have challenged me on this, and I have suggested that their clients should be represented by someone with a more pleasant demeanour. No one deserves to be spoken to offensively. That's not to say that there won't be tense and heated moments throughout the audition process (and particularly in the negotiation stage) between casting director and agent. But we all have a basic duty to be civil to each other. Similarly, agents who are constantly submitting inappropriate suggestions, or send in actors of poor quality, quickly find that their clients aren't seen. If your agent has a reputation for being rude or untrustworthy, I guarantee you will not stand as good a chance as others of being met.

Online casting services

With the phenomenal wealth of internet information, it's worth taking a moment to talk about online casting directories, which are now invaluable to all the major casting directors and are key tools for us to find actors, view pictures and CVs, watch show reels and voice tapes, and find agent details. In the UK, the premier online facility is Spotlight Link (run by Spotlight), in Australia Showcast, and in the US Breakdown Express and

Actors Access. Most online facilities charge a reasonable yearly fee to advertise you; don't begrudge paying for these services as they are vital tools of the trade, and casting directors use them on a daily, if not hourly basis to search for actors.

There are numerous other casting directories available – my personal advice is that if these other services are free, there is no harm in you subscribing to them, but it's currently unnecessary to pay for any other services other than those leading services mentioned above for your respective country. They also provide useful information and services beyond casting.

If you have a personal website, or your agent has a website, that's fantastic, and valuable too as you can make them much more personal, but use these in conjunction with the major online services.

A couple of tips relating directly to online casting directories. I'm basing these points on the UK's Spotlight Link service; the same points apply to any online casting directory service, although some facilities may differ from service to service.

- Update your individual information and credits regularly. There is often a space for you to add general comment at the top of your credits page and it's very helpful for us to see authentic notes such as *'Currently appearing in such and such a production until 13 December 2009'* or *'Nominated for Best Actor in a Musical 2012'*. And more and more in this digital world I'm using online directory CVs in the audition room. If your online profile is not up to date, you may not be telling us about your most recent exciting credit.

- Be truthful. On most directories you're able to give yourself a grading in certain skills. But *don't* say you're highly skilled in doing a regional accent or pointe work or operetta if you're not. And if you can't play the bongos or tap or sing castrato, *don't* say you can.

- Similarly, do say what you *can* do. You never know when that banjo night course may be your lucky break.

- Present a variety of headshots. It gives us a wider sense of what you look like. Show contrasting pictures with hair up, hair down, with and without glasses, with facial hair and clean-shaven, and try to include one full-length shot, particularly if you're a dancer. But remember that your main picture should be your best headshot (see below).

- Take advantage of any additional services such as the inclusion of voice recordings and show reels.

- Be truthful about your height and weight, and update them regularly. Similarly, if you've made drastic changes to your look, then your photos should reflect that change.

How do casting directors decide who to audition from the submissions they receive?

First, you should know that for a major professional musical production, it's not uncommon to receive thousands of submissions, and with this knowledge there is a key point to understand.

> **We will probably only be able to audition a fraction of the thousands of actors who are submitted. This means that if you are fortunate enough to get an audition, it's a privileged, exciting opportunity and one that you must take seriously.**

Once we have all the submissions by the due date, casting directors will painstakingly look through all the CVs and pictures, and decide whether each individual actor has the basic qualities we are looking for in each role as discussed with the creative team. I like to grade my submissions into the following categories:

Yes – A	I definitely want to see this actor
Yes – B	I'll see this actor if I run out of A choices
Wild card	I've got a good instinct about this actor – they're not quite right perhaps on paper but I think they might surprise us
Hold	I'm interested in them but not enough to see them first time round
Rejection	I don't need to consider this actor for this production

Oh no! Only halfway through the first chapter and I've already said the terrifying 'R' word: rejection. I'm afraid that one of the hard facts of our business is that even before you've sung a note, you might be in the 'no' pile. I'll deal with the 'R' word in greater detail towards the end of the book. But for now, there is a possibility you simply won't be called in to audition. If an agent hasn't heard from the casting director following the submissions deadline, and they know other appointments are being set up for other people, they will often call to ask why they haven't had the call yet. You too will almost certainly know fellow actors who have received an audition appointment. Usually there will be a very good reason why we haven't called you in to meet us; either the casting director knows your work and doesn't feel you're suitable (and a good agent will do everything possible to persuade the casting director otherwise) or despite the detailed breakdown, you're the wrong height, wrong look, etc.; you don't fulfil all the criteria of the breakdown. I will normally try to be very clear about why someone isn't in my 'to audition' pile but sometimes, regrettably, it's simply that I can only see 200 people, and with such a vast number of submissions not everyone can be seen. It's the first of many theatrical knocks, I'm afraid. I have to go on my instinct and initial judgement based on the information I have in front of me or have gathered about you. And please don't think that because you're not called in to audition, it means that you're not liked. It just means that the casting director is being very specific about who they want to meet.

If you're a recent graduate, what are the chances of being seen for a principal role?

It very much depends on what the role is, and who you are. There have certainly been actors given leading roles straight out of college, but this is rare. The normal progression would be to work your way up through the ensemble with a leading understudy position attached. It is more likely that we will offer a leading role to an actor who has at least had some professional experience before. But there are exceptions, particularly in smaller-scale, less commercial productions. As ever, it's whether you are perfect for the role that is the prime objective for us, and by exuding confidence and maturity you may well convince us that you're the one who can handle the demanding responsibility that comes with being a leading artist.

Your photographs and CVs

CVs and headshots are vitally important and may make all the difference as to whether you are in the A group, B group or, worst of all, the R group. It may be the first time we 'meet' you, so you must make a great impression.

Photographs

Your visual image, be it in person or your photograph (often referred to as a '10 by 8' or 'headshot'), is vitally important. I landed two jobs entirely on my headshot which, at that point, just happened to fit the rather quirky character breakdown. You should obviously have discussions with your agent and photographer about exactly what you require, but my personal advice would be as follows:

- A professionally shot picture that truly represents you and is *recent*. You should aim to have pictures taken every two or three years. Every year seems to be unjustified unless you have drastically changed your appearance.

- The image should be natural, clear and focused, and show your full head. No moody lighting, no soft focus, not too close so we miss your ears or hair, no excessive touching up, no heavy make-up, no specific sense of character, and no unnecessary body parts taking focus from your face, particularly your eyes.

- The image should have an energy to it. I don't mean an action shot, of course, but a still picture can exude a sense of energy, even though it's a still picture. A good photographer will capture this.

- For the main picture you use, I favour a picture that says 'hire me' without being desperate – this tends to be an engaging but neutral look where the eyes draw the focus. Eyes in pictures are the key to making us look at, and warm to, the face. Eyes need to shine and give a sense of subtle intention.

- Neutral doesn't mean boring, it means it should say a lot of things, suggest a range of emotion.

- You don't necessarily need to smile – although it's refreshing to have an engaging happy open face in a pile of moody, theatrically intense pictures. I think it's interesting if I can't quite tell which way the expression may be going; is that look on the edge of laughter or on the verge of tears?

- Subtle clothing – the colour will be partly determined by background colour, but plain dark shirts/blouses I believe work well, with a collar. T-shirts are fine if they are plain and smart. No large-patterned or logo-filled shirts.

- Good lighting. We want to see all your features without any dramatic shadows.

- There is a specific requirement for dancers to have full body shots, but if you're not a dancer, keep to the headshot. No nudity, please.

- I tend to favour studio shots for theatre work, but I believe TV and film casting directors rather like exterior shots.

- Facial hair (for gents, of course) is fine so long as it's neatly trimmed and looks respectable, or is a permanent feature of your 'look'. If you are more often clean-shaven, then use a clean-shaven picture as your leading picture.

Where do I find a good photographer?

Start by asking your agent or acting colleagues. Have a look in programmes and see what headshots grab you, then try to find out who took the picture. Online searches, of course, and trade magazines and papers all have advertisements.

Is a home computer printout acceptable?

While a professionally duplicated headshot is always going to be best, the quality of home printing is almost as good and considerably less expensive. Be sure that you scan and print at the highest quality you can, and print on good-quality heavy photo paper. These photographs are going to be thrown into folders, pinned on walls and manhandled many times over the course of a long audition process and they can't be on flimsy paper. Also, printing on quality matt paper (rather than gloss) is best as matt paper tends to fax, scan and photocopy better, which is useful when we need to electronically send your photograph on to someone who lives outside the auditioning city. Also, *always* include your name and contact number on the back of the photo in case it gets detached from your CV.

THE CV/résumé

There are many ways to present a CV/résumé, but one classic format and information is shown in the following example.

LEON FERRITHURD

DOROTHY PALMER ASSOCIATES
128 Croxbourne Road, London, WC2 3XY
Tel: 020 7692 3445 Mob: 07968 465 982
email: dorothy@palmerassociates.com

Date of birth: 19 February 1969
Nationality: British
Training: BA Hons Theatre Arts
(Performance),
Middlesex University
Associate of LAMDA,
NYMT
Height: 5" 9' / 175 cm
Weight: 66.5kg / 10 stone 4 lb
Eyes: Brown　　　　**Hair:** Brown

Vocal type: Tenor, high falsetto
Vocal range: Bottom G to falsetto D
Dance: Intermediate Ballet, Jazz, Advanced Tap

THEATRE

ANNIE	Ikes (u/s Rooster)	Victoria Palace, London
Dir. Martin Charnin
COMPANY	Paul	Library Theatre, Manchester
Dir. Roger Haines
LES MISÉRABLES	Ensemble (U/s Thenardier)	Palace Theatre, Lon.
Res Dir. Shaun Kerrison / Ken Caswell
FIDDLER ON THE ROOF	Motel the Tailor	London Palladium and Tour
Dir. Sammy Dallas Bayes
CITY OF ANGELS
(Original London cast)	Angel City Four	Prince of Wales Theatre
Dir. Michael Blakemore
.A JUDGEMENT IN STONE
(Original London cast)	Giles Coverdale	Lyric Hammersmith, London
Dir. Neil Bartlett
OLIVER!	Fagin	Sadlers Wells Theatre, NYMT
Jeremy James Taylor
LITTLE RATS	Mons Petit	Sadlers Wells Theatre, NYMT
Jeremy James Taylor, Mark Pattenden

TELEVISION AND RADIO

THE VAMPYR	Mark	BBC Television, Dir. Nick Finch
THE RAGGED CHILD	Tommy	BBC Television, David Buckton/JJT
TAILOR OF GLOUCESTER	Choir Master	Dreamscape Prods
EASTENDERS	Mike	BBC Television
REBECCA	Lord Arthur	BBC Television
SINGING TOGETHER	Presenter	BBC Television

FILM

AMY FOSTER	Brother Peter	Tapson Steele Prods Dir. Beeban Kidron
COLOUR OF MONEY	Colin Peters	Colour of Funny Prod. Dir. Barry Hemsley
WILT	Student	Channel 4 Films Dir. Michael Tuchner

RECORDINGS

LES MISÉRABLES 10TH ANNIVERSARY CONCERT	Ensemble	First Night Records
RAGGED CHILD	Tommy	First Night Records
CITY OF ANGELS	Angel City Four	First Night Records
LETTERS	Tom	Own Label
THE WILL TO KILL	Anthony	Own Label

Accents:
RP, London, American and Southern, Gen. New York, French, Italian,
Australian, Jewish, South African, Spanish, Welsh, Scottish, Lancashire,
Manchester, West Country

Special Skills:
Piano Grade 8, Oboe Grade 8, Voice Grade 8, Composer and Arranger,
Conductor
Swimmer, BADC Stage Fighting Certificate Level 2

Leon has also appeared in numerous commercials with clients including
Kentucky Fried Chicken, British Telecom, British Midland, Direct Line and
Steigermann

Key information we need to see is:

- your name

- your agent (if you have one)

- your contact details (your agents, or your personal information if not) including postal address, land line, mobile/cell and email

- your date of birth

- your nationality and any current visa information, if necessary

- your physical attributes, including height, weight, hair and eye colour

- your training

- your singing vocal type and range, dance skills, stage fighting awards and other awards which may be of use

- a picture – your leading headshot, about 5cm by 8cm

- union membership

- your credits. There is always consternation about what should go first – theatre, film or TV. In truth, it doesn't matter. There's no standard so long as your credits are a) grouped together and b) in chronological date order. It's important to see a progression of work. Normally film, TV, then stage work well. If you work mainly in theatre, however, then reverse the order and put that first. You may also have a straight theatre and musical theatre subdivision

- your credits should display in columns the production title, your character name or position (ensemble, swing, dance captain), the director and the venue. If you have space, the producer or management is useful too

- additional small credits including commercials, recordings, cabaret at the end

- skills, including accents, sports, acrobatics, circus skills, instruments you might play, etc. Don't go overboard – keep this short and remember to be truthful. I once lied that I could drive, got a television job and then spent the whole day in a car having to be taught how to drive 200 metres. No one was very impressed

- interests – I'm not normally too bothered about whether you can cook a great fish pie or love your nephew, but it's interesting to know that you write music, or have a novel published. Keep these interests art-based.

There may be other important things you want us to know, but the above list covers the essentials.

Overall, keep your CV/résumé

- concise and uncluttered

- easy on the eye – I'm going to be looking at hundreds of CVs per day. Make it easy for me to find what I need quickly

- informative – I want to get a sense of how interesting and versatile you are

- professional – this is your calling card and must properly represent you.

Should I add my training credits?

If you don't yet have enough professional credits, then yes, you should, under the heading of *Roles while in training*. As you build up your work, you can take the training credits off. If you've not trained, then be cautious in adding amateur dramatic roles; it has some relevance for us to see you've played Fagin for the Felton Guild Musical Society, but if you're only twenty-one, we'll have already worked out that it probably wasn't a professional production.

Should I list understudy roles?

This is a contentious question to answer. Some believe you should always state 'understudy' after the role, some don't. I have often seen an understudy be as good as – and sometimes better than – the actor engaged to play the role. I personally believe you don't need to add 'understudy' after a credit if you played the role many times. There will be some who disagree, and so if you want to be more cautious than I'm suggesting, add 'understudy' in brackets after the credit.

Should I include student films?

While participating in a student film shows your accomplishments, I'm afraid some are not very good. I would say as a rule that if you're not proud of it and would be embarrassed if someone asked to see it, then don't include it.

On a long-running show, should I list the original director of the production or the resident director I worked with?

If you were in the nineteenth year of *Les Misérables*, it's unlikely that you were directed by Trevor Nunn or John Caird. However, adding Trevor or John's name says that you meant the production that 'swept the world' in the 1980s and 1990s rather than the newer touring production of 2010. However, if you've added the theatre then we'll know which production it was anyway and therefore it would be useful to have your resident director's name as well in case we want to call up and ask questions about you.

Do you call up past directors and company managers?
Yes, we do – often.

Should I include fringe/off-Broadway credits?
Absolutely, yes. I think there is a point where you begin to hit dangerous territory, but you'll get a sense of the fringe and off-Broadway venues and companies who are respectable and have a reputation for presenting excellent work. It may also be the case that you are cast in leading roles which you may not have the opportunity to play in larger-scale, commercial theatre. That's useful to know about.

What is a casting director looking for on a CV?

If you've followed the advice above and your CV is clear and truthful and you fit the criteria of the breakdown, a casting director is looking for several things:

- We're interested in the productions you've worked on and the roles you've played – it gives us a sense of your performance range.

- We're interested in the people and companies you've worked with – giving us a sense of the quality of your work (although like many things in our profession, that can be subjective).

- We're interested in whether you have West End/ Broadway/long-run or regional touring experience – which may suggest that you have an understanding of the energy, commitment and stamina involved in playing eight performances a week for fifty-two weeks. That's not to say that we would dismiss someone who hasn't yet been in a long-running production. Everyone has to have their first opportunity.

- We're interested in your additional skills, including accents, instrumental skills, gymnastic tricks, etc. – they may be particularly useful in refining who we want for a role.

- We're interested in where you've trained – if, for example, the role is a particularly difficult dance-based one, it's good to see that you've been to one of the colleges which have traditionally maintained a strong level of dance training. That's not to say that we wouldn't see someone with the right skills outside of these colleges; it'll be obvious in the audition whether you have the skills we need. You may be someone who has never trained but has exceptional natural talent. In contrast, there are some who have trained for years but are still awful.

- We're interested in something special about you. I can't really define this but it's something that already sets you apart from the others. It might simply be that the whole package (your CV, picture, credits, etc.) just 'feels right'. I often call these 'wild-card' possibilities. It's an instinct; a 'something' that's indefinable but you just get a good feeling that it's right.

I've heard people say you should have two CVs – is that right?

If you're an actor who wishes to be in musical theatre as well as 'straight' drama, TV or film, then it can be advantageous to have two CVs – one for musical theatre work and one for straight work. It's sad but true that some film and television casting directors have a prejudice against actors who regularly perform in musical theatre and you can help yourself get over that obstacle by having different CVs. There are several problems, the first being that you may not have enough decent individual credits, the second being that on many of the online casting services you can only have one CV, in which case you must include as many good and wide-ranging credits as possible. The same, to some extent, can be said for having different headshots. Your agent will advise you which is best for each scenario.

As well as submissions, we'll also compile a personal list of potential actors. This list will be collated from information we have gathered over the years; actors we've admired and noted from previous productions and workshops, recommendations from various sources, actors we've auditioned in the past, even actors we've met at parties and theatre trips, etc. The potential source is endless.

The casting directors' database

Most casting directors have a database containing vast numbers of records from past auditions. This presents a very important and positive lesson to learn:

You may not get the job you originally came in for but if you've done well in your audition, you will be remembered and are likely to be called for other auditions in the future.

I have a really bad memory and to counteract my amnesia I have a complex database storing audition notes and all kinds of information to help me quickly find actors who have auditioned for me in the past. Whichever method a casting director chooses for the storage of their information, they will remember you for future castings. Directors and other members of the creative team also keep notes; I was recently on a panel for the BBC and the musical director sitting next to me (knowing in advance that I was on the panel) produced my audition notes from an audition I had done for him seventeen years earlier.

Seeing actors in productions

Like agents, casting directors spend a lot of time in the theatre seeing actors in performance. For me, that normally means going to three or four productions a week, and it's a great way to build relationships with agents, and actors too. It's important for me to get to know actors socially, in addition to what you do on stage. I want to build a joyful company, and that drink after the show is a good way to see what you're like as a person as well as an actor. Some casting directors find this uncomfortable and prefer not to socialise. Don't be offended if they don't meet you afterwards; it may be that they have an early casting the next day or they 'just don't do that social thing'. The fact that they've seen you in performance is the most important thing.

I also go to see a lot of performances when I know an understudy is performing, as well as invited understudy performances, workshops and readings.

Regardless of which actor I've specifically gone to watch, I inevitably make brief notes of everyone who's performing, which go into my personal database. There is a rather unprofessional, lackadaisical attitude that engulfs some companies when several leading understudies are performing, where some performers don't give 100 per cent. But beware:

> **Whenever a leading role is being played by an understudy make sure your own performance is perfect as it's highly likely that there may be several casting directors watching.**

In truth, of course, you should always be giving 100 per cent, regardless of who's watching.

Direct submissions from actors

So far we've talked about what your agent does to get you an audition: submissions, calls, nagging, and taking casting directors to see you in productions. But what can *you* do?

I'm always amazed that actors are not more proactive in getting work. There are hundreds of actors I meet who regularly complain about their agent who, apparently, does nothing.

'Haven't heard from them in weeks,' they say, frustrated that the bar work is becoming the main source of yearly income.

'And what have *you* done to find work?' I ask tentatively.

Normally this question results in a look of horror at the thought that something should be done in addition to the work of the agent. But why not? After all, no matter how good your agent is, it remains your responsibility to pay your way through life, not theirs, and so if there are things you can do to complement their work, then do them. Remember that all these extra things you can do are not *replacing* your agent. A good agent won't mind you being proactive, but some agents won't like you doing it behind their backs. Liaise with them and tell them what you're planning to do. A two-pronged attack must surely be better than just one. But do check with your agent to see how the two of you can maximise your opportunities together. If you don't have an agent then self-promotion is of course vital.

Postcards

For every acting job I did, I made postcards which had a picture of me on the front, with my name and agent details, then on the back an invitation to come and see me in my current role, detailing the dates of the production, where it was playing, a space for the handwritten address and a repeat of my agent's details. Occasionally I added review quotes. I would normally print about 200 and send them out to producers, directors and casting directors. That may seem a lot, and you need to make sure your role is worthy of a casting director's trip; not everyone will want to hike a hundred miles to hear you sing six bars. However, a well-designed, good-quality postcard does a number of things:

- It shows that you are proactive, professional and positive about wanting to do well in your profession.

- It tells us what you're doing and when you're available – if I may not be able to get to see you, I will still enter the information into my database.

- It reminds us about you – just having your face flash across our desks every now and then cements you that little bit firmer in our minds. I pin some postcards around my desk or keep them in a quick search box and I flick through that box periodically and find the perfect person for a role I'm currently casting.

Although you may send out over a hundred cards, and get only one or two responses, don't get demoralised; it has not been a waste of time. Even getting one audition out of this exercise is worth the expense. And if one audition results in you signing your next contract, it's been worth it, right?

There are a number of very good online printers who will print full-colour postcards within a couple of days at a very reasonable price. Type 'online printers' into your search engine to see what's around.

A word of warning: if you're self-represented or include your personal contact information, do put your postcard in an envelope. Assuming you have included a picture and an address or mobile number as your contact, you don't want all and sundry witnessing your beauty and having your private contact details, do you? There are some unscrupulous people out there, I'm afraid …

Letters

A personal letter is often an easier and quicker way to get a casting director's attention, but do your homework. No one likes getting a letter which is messy, unprofessional, has spelling mistakes, and suggests that it's one of a thousand impersonal mail-outs. You must ensure that everything you send out represents you in the best professional light. You're a business after all and you must market yourself with diligent care and attention to detail.

So:

- Personally address the letter by name to the casting director at the correct address; ideally the casting director's office address, but if you don't know it, care of the theatre where you saw the production or to the production company.

- Find out what productions the casting director is currently casting for via the internet or other sources, then read the piece or see it (if it's already playing), and reference a specific role you think you might be right for in your letter. Always say something like '*I don't know how you envisage the role being played, but based on my reading of the script, I think I would be right for the role of ...*' This is because the role may not necessarily be cast in the same way as it may have been portrayed in previous productions. It would show an arrogance to assume you know better than the creative team do, but appropriate for you to show that you've read the script and are proactive in associating with a certain character.

- Keep your stationery in neutral colours, on quality paper.

- Insert your photograph on your notepaper; it's easy for you to create stylish notepaper on a home computer and quality printer which includes a good headshot. Remember to give your contact details and include your CV and your large-size headshot (with your name and contact details on the back too). You'd be amazed how many letters I receive with no reply address or phone number. The only address, in this case, is my bin.

- Don't be offended if your letter is not responded to. Answering letters is not at the top of a busy casting director's priorities, although we do try to respond when we can. Better that your letter is put in a 'to be seen' pile and our 'reply' – so to speak – is you coming in to meet us.

- Try to get a professional-sounding email rather than something like 'megabelt@hotmail.com' or 'bustytwinkletoes@yahoo.com'. While it may represent you well, it just sends the wrong message and isn't very professional.

- Check spellings and punctuation.

Emails and cold calls

I don't advise you calling a casting director unless you are agent-less and your enquiry is regarding an audition you have already been scheduled for. Besides, most casting directors require your CV and photograph if we don't know you, and even if you do phone, you'll be asked to send something in. So save the phone call expense. Emails are slightly more acceptable, and in today's environmentally friendly world, I personally prefer to have electronic pictures and CV's rather than by post. However, I still have to print out the actors I'm meeting for the audition, so overall, I do think post is better for me.

Promotional gimmicks

I've had sweets. I've had fridge magnets. I've had mugs with 'mug shots' on them. I've had mouse mats with a headshot from actors called Matt. I've had calendars with an actor's range of roles displayed for each month in various states of undress (you should have seen July; it was a *really* hot summer). I've had any number of bottles, cakes, chocolates, teabags with a picture of the actor on the teabag label and a note to say 'Put your feet up, Neil; have a cuppa on me and read my CV' ... and so on. The best was a holiday, which I didn't accept. Lovely as they all are (and I did say be proactive a little while back, didn't I?), you are selling your talent, not promoting your knowledge of marketing products. Everything I've mentioned above just feels a little desperate. Sondheim's *Gypsy* lyric of 'You gotta have a gimmick' is fine in the audition room (and we will get there in this book, I promise you), and you certainly want to stand out from the crowd. But save your money for singing lessons, dance classes and effective promotional stationery and for when you're out of work. A good, well-written letter, CV and headshot will suffice, so don't waste your money on snazzy and expensive bribes.

Networking

Networking refers to the process of building and maintaining your contacts to help your business acumen by meeting people at various events. The entertainment industry is very social by nature, and while coming into the audition room and displaying your talent is still the main event, a chance meeting with an actor can help focus you in our minds, and who knows what we may be working on that afternoon for which you are perfectly suited? Always say 'hello' to a casting director in the street, at a party, at a workshop, etc. Have your business cards handy, ask what we're casting, tell us what you're doing. Keep the chat friendly and most importantly, be yourself. Don't be someone you *think* you should be in order to impress us. It's likely that we're all in a relaxed, social environment and there's nothing worse than someone trying too hard to be noticed or whose dialogue is forced. This isn't an interview, so keep the chat brief and natural. If it's at a party, there's a chance that we've already had a glass or two so you may need to remind us what you last auditioned for, if we can't remember. We have thousands of names floating around our heads so you may even need to reintroduce yourself. Don't 'hog' us; it's most likely we've been invited by an agent and they won't take kindly to you stealing the limelight from their client.

In the same vein, try to be where directors and other theatrical types hang out. Press-night parties are perfect for networking. I have a dear actor friend who manages to get into every press-night event. I simply don't know how he does it, but he always looks immaculate and graciously 'works the room', saying hi to everyone and being utterly charming. Needless to say he's been in consistent work for almost all the time I've known him. He's extremely talented too but I dare say his ability to network in an unassuming fashion is a huge advantage. People want to work with people they like, and he seems to know, and is adored by, everyone.

Once you've met a director or casting director at a party, and been introduced to other people who may well be of influence, remember the names and send one of your postcards the very next day. '*Dear Neil – It was great to see you last night. So pleased that your productions are going well. I finish* Chicago *on 27 February so it would be lovely to be considered for* South Pacific *recast if you think I'm appropriate …*' etc. *Be proactive.*

Remembering names is really important. There are various books and techniques for remembering names, but if you're as bad as I am, then write them down as soon as possible (and not in front of the person, preferably).

I'm certainly not saying that networking is going to land you a job; I reiterate that it's your talent that will do that and that's the bottom line. But meeting you in a social environment is a nice way to get to know you, and that makes our next meeting in the audition room just that little bit easier and more relaxed.

When networking, know when it's the right time and place. Don't hover, don't butt in, don't be rude, don't be daft. Just wait for the appropriate moment, and be yourself. And don't overstay your welcome!

Reputation

Your reputation is an integral factor to consider, and the creative team aim to bring together a company of people who will work well together and enjoy creating, discovering and performing the show they've been hired to present. Given the huge number of people there are in the business, it's impossible for us to discover everyone's real personality. I've seen companies deliriously happy together as well as companies who have been destroyed by one or two misguided individuals. It's deeply depressing when the latter happens, particularly when that negativity backstage is brought onstage and the whole production suffers.

Of course, there can be many factors that make a job a happy or depressing experience. But please don't underestimate how important your reputation is. I have refused to audition people either simply because someone on the audition panel has had a bad experience working with them before or because they have a poor reputation. You cannot afford to be in that position. It's true that certain artists with an extraordinary talent but with a bad attitude still manage to land roles. The saying 'You'll never work in this town again' is rubbish; I've witnessed producers and directors spit this at an artist with whom there has been some dispute, only to find them hiring the same artist a few years later because they're 'perfect for a role, darling'.

Nonetheless, a clean reputation is like gold dust, and you should do everything you can to leave it untarnished. In most cases it's down to simple respect and good human values.

Of course, you may be a victim of having a bad reputation when actually you've done nothing wrong. One such case happened with a young actor I'd seen on stage who I thought would be perfect for the current production I was casting. I was talking about him to a colleague one afternoon, and suddenly out came this tirade relating to him being unreliable. He had apparently caused a great deal of trouble within his previous company and was considered a 'disgrace to the profession'.

It didn't add up. He was clearly gifted. I decided to call the company manager of the production he'd previously been working on, who confirmed that there had been some bitterness towards the guy, but it had stemmed from a particularly vicious verbal attack from someone else in the company who had a grudge against him and had since been spreading malicious but unfounded rumours. I wanted to be absolutely certain, so I called the actor into my office and spoke to him directly, telling him that I had heard bad things about him and would he like to comment. He was very gracious, although shocked, and said that for an inexplicable reason he'd been the victim of negativity. He'd never retaliated and this had only exacerbated the situation. He didn't know why they felt the way they did, but he suggested that already he felt he was losing out on work because of the rumours concerning his reputation.

Taking everything into account, we decided to make him an offer for the role on the understanding that we believed his story, but that if he lived up to any of the rumours that were circulating about him, he would be dealt with pretty heavily.

Of course, he turned out to be one of the most fabulous cast members in the show. Brilliant in every way, and better. On one occasion he literally saved the production from cancellation when both understudies for a leading role were off sick and, at the point where we were going to cancel the show, he spoke up: 'I can do it. I know I don't understudy that role, but I've learnt it and watched from the wings. I know I can do it.'

And he did – rather wonderfully. The fact that we explored his background, sourced information about him, spoke to him directly and then gave him the benefit of the doubt proved to be beneficial not only for our production, but also for his self-esteem. He has worked consistently since and I've cast him again recently in a new production.

And the ending to the tale? I found out who the person was who started the rumours. They were struck off a recent call-back list and have a black mark by their name in my database.

We do call company managers, general managers, other casting directors, directors and agents if we're concerned about casting someone with a poor reputation. Everyone deserves the opportunity to redeem themselves and if the talent is exceptional, and assuming the references are good and the actor in question knows they're being monitored, then I think most people would take the chance and cast them. As I've said, no one wants a disruptive energy in a company; it's particularly destructive and time-consuming for the company, the company managers and the producers. But be assured that those with undisputed bad reputations will not get seen.

Realistic expectations

I was minding my own business one lunchtime when an actor came up to me.

'You've never seen me for anything,' she said rather aggressively, plonking herself next to me in a spare seat.

'Well, I tried recently but you didn't think the role was big enough and declined to come in.' I continued my beer, hoping she'd go away.

'But I'm a leading artiste,' she grunted. Her CV did not suggest so.

'But you've never had a leading role, to my knowledge.'

'Well, I know I could play *Lady of the Lake*. You never saw me for that!'

'No.' The conversation went downhill from there and my beer went down in one.

The moral is clear. You have to be realistic about the roles you aspire to play. I'm not saying you shouldn't have a crack at a leading character, but clearly being submitted for a role you are not right for (for any number of reasons) suggests a severe lack of understanding.

Nearly time for us to call the agents ...

After all the various submissions, detailed background work, lists and lengthy discussions with the directors and creative teams, we will have our final 'yes' pile – the group of actors we want to meet for each role. It's highly likely that members of the panel will also have suggested their own ideas to add to the final lists – some will cross over with people already scheduled to come in, some we know are not available and some will be new ideas we may simply not have thought of or known about.

And with that full audition list to hand, we'll ring your agent with some good news ...

WORDS OF WISDOM

The Audition Overview

Richard Eyre

When I was an actor I went for an audition for a film commercial. It was for a cigarette called Guards, which featured a guardsman in a bearskin on its packet. As I walked in the door the casting director looked up: 'Too short,' she said. I nodded, turned and left. It might have been short on tact and grace, but it was the fairest and truest of judgements. It had something in common with casting for musicals where the judgements (up to an agreed level) are as objective and as unarguable. After all, there is no possible profit in lying in answer to the questions 'Can you sing?' and 'Can you dance?' And if you are an actor who can sing but has never danced it is easy enough to discover that potential. The late and great choreographer David Toguri used this test: he'd say, 'Walk across the room in time.' He'd click his fingers and within moments, like a musician with perfect pitch, it was possible for him to detect the promise or absence of the ability to move a body in rhythm.

It's that quantifiable aspect of auditioning for musicals that makes it more attractive than auditioning for plays and films. It's altogether less subjective, and if you spend your life sitting alone in small rooms with a casting director, often reading in for other parts yourself, it can be a relief to find that you're just part of a jury composed of producers, choreographers, musical directors, authors, composers and assistants. It's intimidating perhaps for the auditionee, but most musical performers are hardened by their frequent exposure to this system as well as being inherently confident in their musical and physical abilities.

Jerry Mitchell

It seems we are always in auditions. As actors, dancers, singers, directors, choreographers and producers, looking for the perfect match. A casting director spends countless hours finding talent that he or she thinks might be right for the role, then bringing that talent to us hoping to find the perfect match, the actor who fits the material. When that happens it makes everything right. Casting is the beginning of the work. It is so very important for each and every young and upcoming actor to remember auditioning is the norm. It is the only way, the very best way to find the perfect match. As an actor your job is to get in front of the creative people and say, 'Hey, hi! Here I am and if I'm right for this, fantastic, and if not, I had a great time being here today, meeting all of you, and I look forward to seeing you again at a future audition.' That is the kind of attitude I look for when I'm in the audition process. When I'm in any audition I may have more than one project I am working on even if the audition is for a single show. The time you spend in the room is often not just about the audition but all the people behind the table are seeing you for anything and everything they may be working on. So remember the opportunity an audition affords is sometimes bigger than the role you are going in for.

Working on a show is intense. I want to fall head over heels for each and every actor I cast. I have to believe they are the character. If I don't, how can I expect an audience to? We will be spending the next six to eight weeks together trying to make something special happen as we work together to tell a story. I will need their full commitment as well as their talent. I will need their four Ds: Desire, Drive, Discipline and Dedication, making the room a fantastic place to go to every day as we create this story.

Christopher Luscombe

Audition technique always seems to me largely a matter of common sense, but, as we all know, rational thought gets muddled very quickly when the pressure is on.

The important thing to remember is that the director wants you to be The One. He needs to find the right actors, and preferably as quickly as possible. Then there's the casting director, who's praying that he's brought in the best candidates in town. So if you can convince them that you're the man or woman for the job, everyone's a winner.

Attitudes

David Taylor

When the German production of *Cats* was running in Hamburg in the 1980s and 1990s, I had to audition all over Europe for replacements. I was in Rome for one of these auditions and at the dance call – always the first element of the *Cats* auditions – there was one American girl. As the combination was taught, she continually pushed to the front (even after the dance supervisor reversed lines to be fair) and then began to ask rather obvious questions regarding counts. Given that she was one of the best dancers there, this started to be annoying. She seemed to be constantly trying to call attention to herself.

We then moved on to the singing and, having carefully explained that I wanted to hear whatever the actor felt best showed his/her voice and ability, she proceeded to take over half of her allotted time to show us all the pieces she had brought and explain why she was unsure what to sing. Again, the talent was not in question, as she was one of the better singers.

We kept her until the end of the audition and at that point my music and dance supervisors and I all agreed that she was right for at least two roles in the show. However, we all agreed that she would drive us all crazy while she was learning it and take up far too much time when we had twenty performers to teach in a limited amount of time.

Naturally, given her attitude, she came up to me when we cut her. 'So, what was it,' she said, 'the singing or the dancing?' I did consider saying something fairly innocuous but I thought maybe the truth might actually make her consider her situation. 'It was neither the singing nor the dancing,' I answered. 'It was the attitude. You have to trust your talent and our expertise at recognising it. So don't play games and waste time trying to call attention to yourself. If you are good, we will notice. We're professionals and we expect you to be.'

2

PREPARING FOR YOUR AUDITION

The phone rings.

'Hello, darling, it's Dorothy.'

'Dorothy, hi! How's things? Saw you in the TV audience of *Strictly Bum Prancing* last night ...'

'Ahh, darling, gone are the days I could get my lallies behind my head. Still, that's what you're here for, eh? To fulfil my dreams, darling, my dreams. Now, I've got an audition for you, love. I think you'll like it.'

Types of audition

There are various types of musical theatre audition you may attend over the course of an audition process. The order and number of each type of audition will change depending on who is casting the show, who the creatives are, which role you are being seen for and the type of production it is.

- *Pre-meets/preliminaries* – this will generally be a quick solo singing call, possibly with just the casting director or the casting associate/assistant, lasting five or ten minutes, where you will prepare a couple of songs of your own choice. Most likely, you will be called to one of these auditions if the casting director doesn't know you, or hasn't seen you for a while, or wants to hear if you're suitable for the style of the production.

- *An initial singing audition* – this may just be with the casting director, director and the musical director. Again, it may be quite a quick audition (five or ten minutes long) and either you will be asked to sing a song of your choice or you may be sent specific material from the show.

- *A dance audition* – speaks for itself, but a call with probably thirty or so other dancers where you will learn a routine, and then present the routine in smaller groups of three or four to the creative team.

- *An acting audition* – there's a chance you may be asked to read scenes from the production at any point in the audition process, depending on how much spoken text there is in the play and how long the audition process has been planned for – a short audition process will mean we have to do more with you in the early auditions, and so it's likely this call will be combined with the singing call. It's unlikely that you'll be asked to read at the initial audition, which is likely to focus on singing. But, as ever, be prepared and if you get given text in advance, learn it thoroughly. Remember too that the text (and song) you get sent may mean that you are being considered for an understudy position rather than playing the role in your own right. It's a good idea to find this information out via your agent in advance. Rarely, for musicals, will you be asked to prepare your own speech. Again though, having one or two good speeches of your own gives you the advantage.

- *Call-back* – a call-back (recall) refers to any subsequent auditions after your first audition. There can be many, and they can cover a multitude of disciplines: singing, dancing, acting, workshopping, etc. They can also be spread out over a long period of time and may possibly have you paired up with other actors. See Chapter 5 for specifics about call-backs.

- *Workshop auditions* – it's possible, with some new musicals particularly, that you may be part of a workshop audition. This is different to a full-scale 'tryout' workshop of the production, which may rehearse for a couple of weeks and will focus on the material and getting investors and producers interested. An audition workshop could be a day where the members of the creative team want to see how you work with other actors. Workshop auditions are rare, but for new musicals or musicals with a strong ensemble concept, they can be a valuable addition to the audition process.

- *Final call-backs* – the last set of auditions, where we have whittled down all the auditionees to our top choices for each role. It's likely that the producers and general managers will be at this audition, as well as the full creative team.

Getting your audition information

The most obvious thing to remember is always to keep your diary with you (see 'Audition diary' – Chapter 3). Whether you get a call at home or on the move, you need to write the audition information down, gathering all the following information from your agent:

- the date of the audition
- the time of the audition

- the venue for the audition (together with the full address)

- the name of the production

- the role you're auditioning for

- who the director/choreographer/musical director is

- who the casting director is

- what type of audition it is: singing, dancing or acting

- if dance, what shoes you need to take

- what you are required to prepare

- if you have material to learn, where it's being sent – to your agent, your email, your postal address, your touring venue or your partner's address. I know any number of actors whose material was sent to an address other than the one they were at, resulting in them not getting it until the day before the audition and thereby giving them a distinct lack of time to prepare

- who will be on the audition panel

- what you are specifically asked to wear

If your agent doesn't know all of this information, then ask them to get it, as it's all important and helpful in giving you a head start.

Wait! Do you really want the job you're about to audition for?

What? We've just been offered the opportunity to audition and now you're suggesting we might not want it?

I'm not being negative – it's an important thing to consider right at this moment. Despite the hard work of your agent to get you a meeting, for any number of important reasons, following sensible discussion, you may both decide that this role and production is not actually right for you. It may be because of a personal reason; it may be because of a professional reason. The important consideration is that it reflects badly upon you (and your agent) if you waste time by auditioning when you have absolutely no intention of being in the production. If you don't want the job, but just want to be seen by an eminent director, then you're wasting our time. We can see you again in the future, but not now. Remember just how many people we weren't able to see – by accepting your place at the audition, you have prevented someone else from being seen.

Far better to be honest – ask your agent to politely decline the audition for the reason you've discussed, then write a personal note to both the casting director and the director explaining briefly why you were unable to accept their invitation to audition, and hope that they will consider you in the future for other projects.

The day job

Unless you happen to be particularly lucky in life, you'll almost certainly need to have a second income. There's no shame in doing something else alongside your performance career; it's the reality of working in a precarious freelance business and the need to pay the bills.

With your audition date now given, you obviously need to negotiate time off for your audition. Let's spend 'time out' to discuss temp jobs and second incomes.

That second income ought to be:

- something that allows you to pay the rent and bills when you're out of work, relieving the pressure of you having to accept work which you don't really want to take (and thereby making you unavailable when a dream job does come up)

- something that allows flexibility of hours so that you may attend auditions, performances, classes, etc. without arguing with the boss

- managed by an understanding boss who is aware of your acting desires and what that means in terms of your commitment to his/her business

- something that doesn't take so much of your life that you forget to enjoy it

- something that doesn't take so much of your life that you have no time to prepare for your auditions

- something you will enjoy

- something which possibly has relevance to performance or the entertainment industry

Of course, the ideal is something that you're in control of, where there's no boss or company. I supplemented my performance income by writing music for all kinds of different requirements: incidental music, transpositions for friends, arrangements, orchestrations, etc. I also had three jobs with companies who would employ me on short-term, part-time administration contracts. When I was in *Annie* at the Victoria Palace in London, I spent my day working for the technical office at the English National Opera. Over time, I had built up a good knowledge of the company, thereby being 'useful', and was able to dive in and out of employment without needing to give any lengthy explanations. Gaining further knowledge of the technical aspects of theatre also helped me as an actor. I learnt about stage management, lighting, design, negotiation, people management – all completely valuable. And most important, my boss understood that I needed to take time off for auditions.

Your choices may be varied. I know of an actor who makes the most fantastic jewellery. Another actor builds websites. Another teaches. In this way, time is yours to organise as you wish, and of course this can be so important for those last-minute auditions. A difficult boss is a headache if he/she simply doesn't understand why you have to go for a third call-back in the week and will make you stressed before you've even thought about your audition. Often an evening job is better – bar or restaurant work, or theatre ushering (where you can join in the theatrical banter and feel part of it even if you're not actually on the stage). Theatre work is also a great place to hear about auditions. But beware of getting tired if it's an evening job and try to arrange your auditions with your agent so that if you're regularly working late into the night, you avoid having a 10 a.m. audition. Sometimes it's just not possible, but at least your agent can ask.

Where is your audition being held?

Auditioning in a theatre, a church, a rehearsal space, a dance studio, a car park (yes, I really did once) will inform what you wear, your choices of audition material, even your warm-up possibilities. It's really crucial that you know your audition environment.

Who's going to be at the audition?

Not everyone will be at all the audition rounds, but the key people are:

- *the casting director,* who coordinates the casting process

- *the director,* who has overall artistic vision of the project

- *the choreographer,* responsible for the musical staging and choreography

- *the producer,* whose company will put on the production and fund the venture

- *the general manager,* who will run the day-to-day elements of the production (and may or may not work directly for the producer)

- *the assistant director,* who assists the director

- *the assistant choreographer,* who assists the choreographer and will most likely teach the routines at the dance audition.

- *the music supervisor,* who has overall responsibility for the musical elements of the production

- *the musical director,* who will continue with the responsibility for the musical elements after the music supervisor has left the production and will most likely conduct the musical.

That's already nine people, and then there may also be designers, associates, assistants and co-producers. I have been in auditions with a panel of over twenty people, and that can be hugely intimidating. But remember that everyone wants you to succeed; see them all as friends and you'll soon overcome any worries.

Gathering background information

When I started performing, the internet didn't exist, and at best it meant getting a recording of the production from the library, together with some sheet music, and studying it. Today, you have an incredible wealth of information at your disposal: background information, clips of music, possibly clips of video, and certainly song lyrics and even scripts. When we were casting *Guys and Dolls* for the 2005 revival in London's West End, it was incredible how many auditioning actors didn't know anything about the show other than the title. There's no excuse not to know about the production you're auditioning for (unless of course it's a new musical).

Before auditioning, find out as much as you can about the musical, the creative team, the writers, the production company, this particular production, etc. A good knowledge of the piece, and style, is important.

In terms of the piece, find out:

- who wrote it
- other songs you may also know by the writers
- the style of musical theatre

- any historical background you can – did it break boundaries in musical theatre writing?

- if there's a recording of the show, just to give you a feel of the style of music, although beware of two things relating to show recordings:

  A cast recording may not accurately represent the music you have been sent. It may have cuts, it may be in a different key, the orchestration may be totally different from the piano sheet.

  If the production is a newly revived production, it may well be that there's a new concept. It's quite possible new songs have been written and older songs deleted. So while there will be some use in listening to the recording, this particular production may be very different. Finding this out in advance from the casting director or agent is important.

Find out what you can about the creative team:

- What have they done before?

- Have you met any of them before?

- Have they recently won any prestigious awards?

- Have you seen any of their work on stage? It's terribly flattering if you can say to the director, 'I loved your production of such-and-such. Really fabulous, congratulations on the Tony Award.' But be sure you really did see it – it would be embarrassing if you were asked a question which you couldn't answer

- What are they currently involved with?

- Similarly with the producers and casting directors,

what have they worked on before? What else do they produce/cast?

All of this information is subsidiary to your audition, and it's highly unlikely anyone will ask you in which theatre on Broadway the original production played, and for how many performances. But by having some solid information in your head, you're more prepared (that word again, yes) than others and in that extraordinary moment when a director happens to ask your opinion or reaction to the production, you will appear to have taken the trouble to do your homework. Besides, as a professional musical theatre performer, shouldn't you take an interest in learning about the genre's heritage in order to progress and continue your learning? And why? Because ...

> ... **without any doubt, the most important thing in addition to having the talent is PREPARATION, PREPARATION, PREPARATION.**

You will see the word *preparation* appear time and time again throughout the book, together with countless tips and advice as to how to prepare effectively. Preparation is the underlying key to helping you on your way to success and covers so many aspects of the audition process, from keeping yourself in good health, physically and mentally, to preparing your audition material, to having a good knowledge of your craft both historically and practically, and so on. Your audition will last only a few minutes. Your preparation will last a lifetime. If you take one word away from this entire book, *preparation* is what it should be.

Your repertoire songbook

Your songbook (portfolio of your songs) is without doubt one of the most important audition tools for the musical theatre performer. It will contain various styles of the songs which you have chosen to perform in front of the panel with the key aim that you'll present them so brilliantly that you'll be asked back to audition again at a call-back.

Your preparation and the subsequent in-depth homework you achieve with your songbook goes a long way to getting you through to the call-back stage. Well-considered, inventive audition songs, which you know thoroughly inside out and show off all aspects of your talent, will have you sailing through the first rounds if you present them well. If you make a poor choice, no matter how good your talent, you risk being rejected at the first hurdle. And the more time you spend finding your material, and the more versatile it is, the more useful that song will be to you.

So, where to start?

Choosing your songs

Even if you're a seasoned professional, please don't skip this section – the majority of auditions fall apart because someone brings inappropriate and ill-prepared music into the first audition rounds. If you haven't looked through your repertoire songbook for a while, maybe it's time for a spring clean.

Let's just remind ourselves what the purpose of these audition songs is. It's not about performing your party piece or singing your favourite song. Neither are you building the list of songs for your first album release. You are auditioning for a specific production, so we have slightly different criteria to consider.

Song styles

Take a look at the current listing of professional musicals and you'll probably find something spanning every decade in the last fifty years. You need to be ready to audition for all of them. You may not like all the genres, but it's not enough in today's competitive world just to be able to sing in one style. You may also feel more comfortable singing in one style over another, but you need to be able to perform a variety of genres if you want to help your chances of being regularly in work.

Below are the main styles, eras and genres, and the key composers writing within those periods. I was slightly conflicted about whether I should provide you with vast lists of song choices; in the end I've decided that it's more important for you to discover your song choices for yourself. Therefore at the end of each section, I list specific composers who I believe best represent each category, together with some of their key pieces for you to explore. The list – while subjective – is not exhaustive and I will almost certainly have left out some of your favourites. Nor do I make any suggestion that each of the writers *only* wrote in the styles under which they are listed; far be it from me to 'box' such wonderful talents. I do so here in this generalised form simply to help you make certain choices.

You should aim to include in your singing portfolio an up-tempo number and a ballad from each of the following categories:

1. Operetta and light opera

This genre is most likely to consist of music from between the late Victorian and Edwardian periods, or from early musicals which cross over between opera and more popular music of the period. George and Ira Gershwin's *Porgy and Bess*, for example, could be argued to be in this category as well as shows like Noël Coward's *Bitter Sweet*. You could also take a peek at the music of Franz Lehar such as *The Merry Widow*.

Most of these musicals require you to have a 'legit' voice – a pure, almost operatic sound, and will probably mean you have to be accurate with your timing and intonation. Of course, that applies to all singing, but some later periods and styles can employ more modern vocal techniques and tricks allowing you to be 'free' in your interpretation. Such 'vocal styling' should not be used for this period of writing.

If you do have a voice that can be classed as 'classically legit', please, please, please don't ever lose it. No matter how strong the temptation and demand to develop other more commercial and modern sounds to your voice (and you should absolutely try to widen your range of singing styles), always keep working on your legit voice as it's becoming more and more rare to hear a decent lyrical tenor or a true soprano. I'm not necessarily talking about an operatic voice but a voice that can beautifully handle a lyrical melody. Don't think that musicals written today are just about pop and rock voices; they are absolutely not and there are some beautiful original scores now being written by new young composers which require voices just as lyrical as were required over fifty years ago.

You may also include in this category modern writing, but that which clearly crosses the divide between musicals and opera. For example, I would urge you to look at Bernstein's opera *A Quiet Place* with a libretto by Stephen Wadsworth (and based on Bernstein's earlier one-act work, *Trouble in Tahiti*), or his other crossover pieces such as *Candide*. Both have terrific examples of arias which could be used for more legit auditions. One could also argue that scores such as *Les Misérables, West Side Story, Phantom of the Opera* or *Sweeney Todd* are 'operatic' in their writing. I personally believe they nod respectfully in the direction of opera in terms of their writing, but for ease of categorising our songs, we'll include them in later categories.

W. S. Gilbert and Arthur Sullivan
  The Mikado
  The Pirates of Penzance
  HMS Pinafore
  and any of their Savoy operas

Noël Coward
  Bitter Sweet
  Sail Away
  After the Ball
  Pacific 1860

Franz Lehar
  The Merry Widow

Leonard Bernstein
  A Quiet Place
  Trouble in Tahiti
  Candide

George and Ira Gershwin (who also appear later)
  Porgy and Bess

John Gay
  The Beggar's Opera

Lionel Monckton and Howard Talbot
  The Arcadians

Lionel Monckton
  The Quaker Girl

2. Pre-Golden Age

The era which many refer to as the Pre-Golden Age covers music which was predominantly written for the stage around the mid-1920s to late 1930s. Some of those works cross over into the jazz styles and the Golden Age itself, but some stand alone as being the early forerunners of what we now recognise as musicals as opposed to operettas. They include the work of George and Ira Gershwin, Rodgers and Hart, Kurt Weill and Cole Porter, to name but a few, and were often 'party pieces' for the star performers of the time, containing minimal plot. There were exceptions, but on the whole these light-hearted entertainments were frivolous and fun.

More often than not, these songs are such that they can be lifted from the show without any interruption to the flow of the flimsy storyline's narrative and are often referred to as 'vertical' songs. Indeed, many composers of the period put songs into their shows which may have been intended as stand-alone songs and not originally part of a musical. So long as their lyrics sounded about right in terms of where the plot had got to at that point in the show, it wasn't a huge concern that many didn't advance the plot during the musical number (a forerunner, possibly, of the back-catalogue musicals of the 1990s). As such many of these songs probably don't have much acting range and are often fun and frivolous, although there are some terrific ballads from this period too. That's not to say they shouldn't be used, but they are probably fairly limited in presenting your emotional acting range. In the audition room you may need to give them a context which might be different from their originally intended placing within the musical. We'll discuss *context* shortly as it's hugely important.

George and Ira Gershwin
Girl Crazy
Of Thee I Sing
Lady be Good
My One and Only
Crazy for You
Strike Up the Band

Cole Porter
> *Paris*
> *Anything Goes*
> *Out of This World*
> *Gay Divorce*
> *Dubarry was a Lady*
> *Jubilee*
> *Leave It to Me*

Jerome Kern
> *Oh Boy!*
> *Sally*
> *The Cabaret Girl*
> *Music in the Air*
> *Showboat* (although technically from the Golden
>   Age)
> *The Cat and the Fiddle*

Vincent Youmans
> *No, No, Nanette*
> *A Night in Venice*
> *Tea for Two*

Richard Rodgers and Lorenz Hart
> *On Your Toes*
> *Babes in Arms*
> *The Boys from Syracuse*
> *Pal Joey* (again, technically from the Golden Age)
> *I'd Rather be Right*

Ivor Novello
> *The Dancing Years*
> *King's Rhapsody*
> *Perchance to Dream*
> *Glamorous Night*

Kurt Weill
> *One Touch of Venus*
> *The Threepenny Opera*
> *Happy End*
> *Lady in the Dark*
> *Street Scene*

Sandy Willson
> *The Boy Friend*

Julian Slade
> *Salad Days*

3. The Golden Age

While many of the composers mentioned above contributed greatly to works included in what is known as the Golden Age of musicals, it's fair to say that there was a noticeable change in the way shows were written during the 1940s, 1950s and early 1960s. Pioneered by Rodgers and Hammerstein, who picked up where Kern had left off with *Showboat*, we began to see musicals which had a cohesive plot, and songs which furthered the action of the plot and character development. Rather than opening a show with a formulaic scantily clad bevy of girls, *Oklahoma* opened with a lone a cappella male voice, offstage: 'Oh, What A Beautiful Morning'. A brave new era in musical theatre was born.

Many of the songs from this period of work provide some of the greatest audition songs, in my opinion, and afford opportunities for you to sing the most beautiful soaring melodies while also allowing you to invest in detailed acting choices. Well-chosen songs from this period will prove to be some of your most valuable material in your repertoire, so choose well.

Do not be afraid to use music from the famous shows of this period. (I could listen to 'If I Loved You' time and time again – so long as it's done well, of course.) Due to the vast range of superb audition material from this period, be sure to choose songs that fit your voice and character well, and showcase your acting ability.

Richard Rodgers and Oscar Hammerstein
Oklahoma
South Pacific
The Sound of Music
Me and Juliet
State Fair
The King and I
Flower Drum Song
Cinderella

Alan J. Lerner and Frederick Loewe
Brigadoon
My Fair Lady
Camelot
Paint Your Wagon
Gigi

Frank Loesser
Guys and Dolls
How to Succeed in Business without Really Trying
Most Happy Fella
Green Willow
Pleasures and Palaces
Where's Charlie?

Leonard Bernstein (with Betty Comden and Adolph Green)
On the Town
Wonderful Town
West Side Story (with lyrics by Stephen Sondheim)

Jerry Bock and Sheldon Harnick
Fiddler on the Roof

She Loves Me
The Apple Tree

Richard Adler and Jerry Ross
The Pajama Game
Damn Yankees

Irving Berlin
Annie Get Your Gun
Call Me Madam

Cole Porter
Kiss Me, Kate

Burton Lane, E. Y. Harburg and Fred Saidy
Finian's Rainbow

Meredith Willson
The Music Man
The Unsinkable Molly Brown

4. The jazz/swing standard

This music is most likely to have come from either the 1940s, 1950s or 1960s and may have been written for the stage or for musical films of the period or, indeed, may be from the popular music catalogue. The bulk of the albums by singers such as Frank Sinatra, Dean Martin and Bobby Darin will provide you with lots of material, as well as the torch songs and swing numbers by Ella Fitzgerald, Billie Holiday and Judy Garland. Don't neglect more contemporary artists such as Michael Bublé, Harry Connick Jnr and Jamie Cullum, who also write in the jazz/swing idiom. You could also look at musicals which are written later than the golden period of jazz, but which have a jazz score, such as Cy Coleman's *City of Angels*.

A word of warning about jazz songs – because they come from a rather specific period of writing and you are most likely to discover them by hearing the great crooners sing them, be careful that you don't present vocal impersonations. If you listen to the famous jazz and swing standards sung by a variety of people, you'll be hard pressed to hear any one song sung the same way. You should also aim for your own performance rather than someone else's (this of course applies to all songs regardless of the period – we never want to hear impersonations). What I strongly suggest is that you learn the song strictly as it's written, and then give yourself the freedom to 'play' with it within the expectations of the style.

Writers whose material you should consider include:

Bart Howard
Billy Rose
Cole Porter (jazz work as opposed to his other musical
    scores below)
Cy Colman (jazz work as opposed to his other musical
    scores below)
Duke Ellington
E. Y. Harburg
Harold Arlen
Johnny Mercer
Jules Styne
Walter Gross
Willie Stein

5. 1960s and 1970s musical theatre

Generally, the musical theatre writing from this period was not necessarily stylised to rock or pop idioms (although of course these styles existed within the popular music charts at the time). Neither was it in the same style as the Golden Age; rather more a continuation of nostalgic traditions but with a nod towards the modern music of the day. There is a whole range of brilliant writing during this period which will be hugely useful within your repertoire.

John Kander and Fred Ebb
The Rink
Cabaret
And the World Goes Round
The Happy Time
The Act
Flora the Red Menace
Kiss of the Spider Woman
Chicago

Jerry Herman
Hello, Dolly!
Milk and Honey
La Cage aux Folles
Mack and Mabel
Mame
Dear World
From A to Z

Tom Jones and Harvey Schmidt
The Fantasticks
I Do! I Do!
110 in the Shade

6. Rock and roll/pop

With musicals such as *Smokey Joe's Café*, *Grease*, *Pump Boys and Dinettes*, *The Rocky Horror Show* and many others of a similar style (and spanning several decades) it's necessary to have at least one or two rock and roll songs up your sleeve. They can either be taken from shows with a rock and roll style, or from the repertoire of singers of the period such as

Elvis Presley, Buddy Holly, Frankie Valli, Little Richard, the Temptations, etc., or later artists such as Meat Loaf, the Who, Queen and Billy Joel. The list is endless. Be aware, however, of keeping the songs that have acting possibilities at the front of your mind as they will be more useful than those which don't. Shows with rock scores such as *Hair, Jesus Christ Superstar, Spring Awakening*, the Who's *Tommy*, etc. all have narrative- and character-specific elements to their songs and so it's wrong to assume that you won't need to show off your acting skills while working on your rock material. You'll normally be told by the casting office whether they specifically want a rock standard (i.e. a song which did not originate from musical theatre) or something from a show.

Some shows (often referred to as jukebox musicals) also require impersonations of their leading characters – *Jersey Boys, Buddy, The Roy Orbison Story*, for example, all contain actors who have to impersonate real people. Others, such as *All Shook Up, Good Vibrations, Dreamboats and Petticoats*, suggest a very definite style of singing in relation to the popular music from which the score derives. If you're being put up for one of those impersonating roles, you need to be doubly sure you a) sound and look like the person you will be required to impersonate and b) are able to replicate that impersonation eight performances a week. You may be able to sing like Frankie Valli in a karoke booth once a year, but to play the role eight times a week requires specific stamina and natural ability.

In terms of musical theatre pop repertoire (which can span the period from mid-1960s up to the present day), there is a plethora of songs to choose from: either pop songs that originate from outside of the musical theatre field, or musical scores that have a pop idiom. The works of Stephen Schwartz, Maltby and Shire, and Stephen Flaherty, for example, all take reference from the pop music of the day, but also – within their musical context – are written specifically with focus on character and plot. As with jazz songs, I would advise you to avoid songs that don't have some acting narrative. You may be specifically asked *not* to sing something from a musical, rather from the musical charts of the period.

One final word on the pop and rock repertoire: many pop/rock songs sound phenomenal on guitars, keyboards and drums but actually shocking on a piano. They may also be poorly transcribed, with few chord symbols, and pianists may simply not understand the 'feel' of the style. Please try to hear your music played on a piano *before* you audition so you know how different it sounds. It can be completely daunting and off-putting if you have this great rock 'vibe' in your head, and instead an insipid piano chord structure is the best you hear. It won't necessarily be the pianist's fault. It's just that he may not be able to re-create the feel you are used to.

Rock and roll:

Queen
   We Will Rock You

Stephen Schwartz and John-Michael Tebelak
   Godspell

Galt MacDermot, Gerome Ragni and James Rado
   Hair

Galt MacDermot, John Guare
   Two Gentlemen of Verona

Pete Townsend
   Tommy

Richard O'Brien
   The Rocky Horror Show

Mark Hollmann, Greg Kotis
Urinetown

Laurence O'Keefe
Bat Boy
Legally Blonde

Jonathan Larson
Rent
Tick, Tick ... Boom!

Pop/contemporary musical theatre:

Stephen Schwartz
Pippin
Working
Children of Eden
The Baker's Wife
Wicked

William Finn
Falsettoland
A New Brain
The 25th Annual Putnam County Spelling Bee

Alan Menken
Little Shop of Horrors (with Howard Ashman)
Sister Act (with Glenn Slater)

Richard Maltby and David Shire
Big – The Musical
Starting Here, Starting Now
Closer than Ever
Baby

Tim Rice, Björn Ulvaeus and Benny Andersson
Chess
Mamma Mia!

Marvin Hamlisch
> *A Chorus Line* (with lyrics by Edward Kleban)
> *They're Playing Our Song* (with lyrics by Carole
> > Bayer Sager)
> *The Goodbye Girl* (with lyrics by David Zippel)

Willy Russell
> *Blood Brothers*

Marc Shaiman
> *Hairspray* (with Scott Wittman)

Writers whose work is chart-based rather than from musical theatre, but whose songs provide good narrative or dramatic context:

> Billy Joel
> Elton John
> Linda Ronstadt
> Meat Loaf
> Burt Bacharach
> John Lennon and Paul McCartney
> Roy Orbison
> Elvis Presley
> Carole King
> George Harrison

7. Stephen Sondheim

I hope you'll allow me to indulge my admiration of this composer by giving Mr Sondheim his own category. As with Rodgers and Hammerstein II, I believe Stephen Sondheim's work is iconic for having taken musical theatre into important new realms of possibility. His style, as with any art, is controversial; some people like it, some people don't. His material is brilliantly inventive, but both musically and lyrically, the songs are often challenging. I do believe that if you can successfully present a Sondheim song in an audition, then you stand to do well.

There are some casting directors and teachers who would advise that you should never do a Sondheim song for an audition. So long as you take into consideration the points below, I believe you should. The wealth of material is huge and exciting, from soaring emotional ballads to incredibly funny and witty point numbers. His work encompasses many different styles as well as giving you incredible source material to show off your acting skills. But these are challenging songs and you *must* work hard on them. When I worked on the casting for the UK production of *Sondheim on Sondheim* I was staggered by how many leading actors came in and fell apart, not having prepared Sondheim songs well enough.

You absolutely must, in my opinion, have at least two contrasting well-chosen, well-prepared Sondheim songs within your audition repertoire. There are, however, some things to be aware of when considering what to use.

- Don't choose something where the piano part is fiendishly difficult. While it's likely that for most professional productions your pianist will be able to play it, it won't do you any favours if they can't. If you feel the song is perfect but you know the piano part is difficult, consider asking an arranger to make the piano part simpler for auditions.

- Be absolutely certain of the melody line – there is often dissonance (in simple terms, harmonic and melodic structures that might sound wrong and need resolution) and you want to be certain that you are singing the correct written note even if it sounds odd. If the panel know the piece, it will be a dead giveaway that you've not learnt your material correctly, which suggests you are lazy.

- Lyrically, Sondheim can be incredibly tricky. Be accurate, and if the song is a patter song – a song with a lot of quick and complicated words – be sure to know them inside out and deliver them with confidence.

Some Sondheim scores you should acquaint yourself with and choose material from include:

> *A Funny Thing Happened on the Way to the Forum*
> *Company*
> *Follies*
> *Sweeney Todd*
> *Into The Woods*
> *Assassins*

(Yes, I know there are many others, but I believe these present a good cross-section of Sondheim's work.)

8. The British and European musicals of the 1980s and 1990s

The 1980s saw the invasion of the 'Euro-musicals' with works from, effectively, two composers – Andrew Lloyd Webber and Claude-Michel Schönberg – and their major collaborating lyricists of the period; with Lloyd Webber, Tim Rice, Charles Hart, Richard Stilgoe and Don Black as well as T. S. Eliot, and, with Claude-Michel, Alain Boublil and Herbert Kretzmer.

Of course, the Lloyd Webber/Rice collaboration had already delivered exciting works such as *Jesus Christ Superstar* and *Evita*. But as successful as those pieces were, it was *Cats, Starlight Express, Phantom of the Opera, Les Misérables* and *Miss Saigon* that catapulted European musical theatre into record-breaking, lengthy runs over the next twenty years in Europe, on Broadway and throughout the world. This was truly the beginning of musical theatre hitting massive commercial heights. They have brought the musical form to millions of people throughout the world, as well as having given employment to huge numbers of actors.

Their massive worldwide popularity does pose one problem, however, in terms of choosing audition songs. Many of the hit songs have become international 'anthems' and have been recorded by many major artists throughout the world. This makes it incredibly difficult to be impartial when trying to judge someone's talent in an audition room.

My advice is, therefore, to be cautious in your choice of material from this category. As with Sondheim, there is a wide range of excellent song material you can choose from, and the styles vary considerably. But try to choose those which are less well known than the obvious standards. Of course, as I've said before, I don't mind hearing a song for the umpteenth time in a day if it's performed brilliantly. But better to avoid one of these hit songs if you can. It's not that they are bad songs – most of them are excellent. It's just that they are too often heard, whether inside or outside the audition room.

9. Animated film musicals

Along with those 1980s Euro-musicals came the emergence of the animated film musical, which started with *Beauty and the Beast* in 1994, followed by *The Lion King*, *Aïda*, *Tarzan*, *Mary Poppins* and *The Little Mermaid*, and more recently *Shrek* and *Spiderman*. Much of this writing is for a unique market and genre, and in my opinion is not always suitable as good audition material. When you're seeing your sixty-eighth actor of the day, and there's another song about being a disillusioned mermaid, or a prince with a curse, or the delights of being an all-singing all-dancing acrobatic dinner plate ... well, it can make you wish you'd listened to your mother and become a doctor. At least then you'd have a quick remedy on hand for nausea and headache.

Before I get accused of being a Wicked Old Queen and get turned into a frog, my brief point is simply that a lot of these songs have very little human narrative, are rarely useful in expressing a full range of emotion and may have limited vocal possibilities. There are exceptions, of course, so again, please just choose carefully. Ask yourself, 'What is this song actually doing for me – is it showing off my acting abilities?' Look through the following checklist of what an audition song needs to deliver, and if it's not delivering, then best look for something else. I'm not saying these songs are poor songs; many are great. I'm saying they have to work for the audition environment and for you to show all your skills.

10. And all the others …

Of course, there are many, many writers throughout the hundred years or so of musical theatre history who I've not mentioned above, along with thousands of shows. I hope you understand that there are simply too many to mention within this book.

However, notable modern musical theatre composers/ songwriters who I feel really do deserve a mention, are my personal favourites, and who you might also investigate, include:

- *Jason Robert Brown* – although with significant cuts for audition songs and with cautious consideration; many of Jason's excellent songs are either too long, or too contextually specific to the piece from which they come, which can be dangerous in auditions.

- *Adam Guettel* – one of my favourite scores is *Light in the Piazza*, a glorious mix of opera pastiche and ingenious musical theatre writing.

- *Stephen Flaherty* and *Lynn Ahrens* – *Ragtime* is another of my favourites.

- *Duncan Sheik* and *Steven Sater* – responsible for the outstanding musical revitalising of *Spring Awakening*

- *Brenda Russell, Allee Willis* and *Stephen Bray* – the songwriters of *The Color Purple*.

- *Zina Goldrich* and *Marcy Heisler* – while not as prolific as others in terms of full works, Zina and Marcy have a wonderful catalogue of musical theatre songs – often very funny and wonderfully clever.

- *Robert Lopez* and *Jeff Marx* – the musical minds behind *Avenue Q*.

- *Janet Hood* and *Bill Russell* – whose score for *Elegies for Angels, Punks and Raging Queens* has some exceptional audition material.

- *Tom Kitt* and *Brian Yorkey* – *Next to Normal* has a wonderful mix of styles.

- *Tom Lehrer* – not a musical theatre writer, but provides some quirky audition material when used for the right audition.

- *Bobby Cronin* – who is writing tremendously exciting fresh work

11. Specialist songs

In addition to the styles above, it's also a good idea to be familiar with:

- a patter song – a fast song characterised by a rapid succession of rhythmic patterns in which each syllable of text corresponds to one note

- a funny musical hall or vaudeville song

- an unaccompanied folk song

You never know when you may need one!

It's your duty as a life-long scholar and lover of musical theatre not just to be able to perform, but to build your knowledge of the history of musical theatre. You should dive into the plethora of work from the last hundred years with great excitement, joy and anticipation, and immerse yourself in every style and nuance that the musical theatre repertoire has to offer. If you hear a song you like that's new to you, write it down and try to find it. If you see a show and you like a number, write it down and add it to your portfolio. Build your tastes, talk to colleagues about their new discoveries (although don't be surprised if they're not keen to share too much with you when they've found something special).

These songs are your audition meal ticket, so make sure they are absolutely right for you, your voice, your personality, your character and your sensibility. If you've done your homework and studied at least those composers and shows I've mentioned above, as well as conscientiously chosen at least two contrasting songs from each category, you should be well on your way to having an excellent and useful repertoire of songs for all audition scenarios.

What makes a good audition song?

Audition songs have certain requirements:

- *A song should last around two minutes.*

- *It should immediately grab the panel's interest and attention from the outset* – in a first-round audition, you may only have three to five minutes to prove yourself worthy of getting a call-back, so make sure your song engages us immediately. Don't waste time on lengthy piano introductions; let's hear your voice as soon as possible.

- *It should show off as many of your talents as possible* – this is difficult as not many two-minute songs can show all your skills and range of vocal quality, but see if you can include as many as possible. Be sure of choosing songs that are *within* your talents – a hugely complex song that stretches you beyond your capabilities should be worked on in advance until it's second nature. You should aim to stretch yourself, absolutely, but do so with your vocal coach and not for the first time in an audition.

- *It must be in your vocal range* – yes, I'm afraid so many people come in with songs that have notes they just can't reach.

- *It must provide an acting narrative* – each song should have a sense of narrative, or at least (if it's a pop, country song or jazz standard) allow you to add your own context in order to achieve a sense of narrative and drama. Remember, if you're singing for a musical audition, it's not *just* about your voice; it's about singing *and acting* as the character within a dramatic context.

- *It should be appropriate for you, the actor* – we want to see a bit of your own personality in your initial audition round, so find songs that make sense to you as well as your character, which will allow you to express and engage within the song. And be aware of descriptive lyrics that go against your physical appearance.

- *It should be appropriate for the character you are auditioning for* – if your character is uplifting, cheery, in love, etc. you will do yourself no favours in singing a suicidal dirge.

- *Choose a song within the period of the production for which you are auditioning* – singing a rock song for a Rodgers and Hammerstein musical is obviously foolish and says a lot about you as a performer. Personally, I wouldn't even let you sing it and would ask you to come back another day with something more appropriate.

- *It should allow you to be imaginative and inventive* – interpretation and context is an interesting discussion in itself which I'll address in the coming pages; but showing a degree of imagination in your song choices rather than presenting a standard version makes us sit up and pay special attention.

- *It may include text/dialogue* – only a little, but it's nice to hear how you handle the technique of speech to song.

- *All songs should contrast and provide variety against other songs in your repertoire.* You will almost certainly be asked to show a contrast in your audition pieces, so don't have too many songs in your repertoire that sound the same.

- *It should be a song you enjoy performing and it should give you confidence* – don't choose songs you hate. Chances are if you enjoy singing it, we'll enjoy listening to you.

- *It should demonstrate your ability as a musician.* You should choose a song that shows that you can stay in tune, have a good rhythmic sense and can stay on pitch, even if the piano part wasn't there and you were singing on your own (a cappella). It's possible that the pianist may stop playing for some reason. You must still hold your ground as if nothing has happened so that when he comes back in, you're still in the same key, and tempo.

What songs shouldn't you sing?

- *Don't sing your karaoke favourite.*

- *Don't sing something from the show you are auditioning for, unless you are specifically asked to.*

- *Don't sing songs in a foreign language unless you are asked to.*

- *Avoid songs which have a few places where the panel can say 'STOP!'* Some songs just need to be sung all the way through to show you off at your best. Most people on the panel will not be rude and stop you mid-vocal (unless you're doing something really awful); they'll generally wait until a solo piano moment. Therefore, don't choose a song that has too many instrumental breaks in it.

- *Don't sing a song where you're constantly aware of the technical difficulties.* If your mind is more focused on how you're going to get that top B♭, rather than on 'being in the moment' dramatically, then it's the wrong song for you. If you've prepared properly and have learnt your songs well, you shouldn't be worrying about any technical difficulties during the song. Believe me, an auditionee who is worried about the technical aspects of the song might as well have a neon sign saying 'Don't Hire Me' above their head. It's that obvious.

- *Don't sing a song that is boring or earnestly self-indulgent.* Something which takes for ever to show off your skills, and is terribly slow and doesn't say much, means we probably won't say much about you either. Bear in mind we may have been sitting there for hours already, it's hot, the mind wanders, and the last auditionee has left the panel wondering what's for supper. Another boring song will, I'm afraid, have the producers snoozing at the table.

• *Don't sing something that you can't handle emotionally.* One must, as an actor, dancer and singer, retain control of emotion and not allow it to take you over completely. If you are out of control of your emotion within a song (and I don't just mean 'upset'; it could be 'anger', 'frustration', 'joy', etc.) you can completely destroy your performance. If you are 'in the moment' as an actor and you cry, that's fine (in fact it can be electric in an audition) but you must maintain your sense of performance control. And, of course, you must know how to replicate that same emotion eight times a week. I've seen sensational, emotionally charged performances in an audition room which have never been replicated as well on stage.

• *Don't sing anything that is too difficult for your pianist.* Part of this comes with experience and the pianist will certainly tell you if your song's a nightmare to play (if you haven't already discovered by him stopping every eight bars). You should have checked in advance during your preparation sessions, of course, and made adaptations. That doesn't mean you can't sing some of the great songs simply because the accompaniment is hard. See if there are other options, easier arrangements, or invest in someone writing a simpler accompaniment for you. A good arranger can do so without affecting the overall 'feel' of the piece.

• *Avoid songs that are overdone.* If you know that the panel regularly hear the same songs being sung, or a song is particularly well known at the moment (perhaps the show's just opened, or it's a hit film theme tune), put it in the drawer for the moment. Songs come in and out of fashion all the time, which is why I'm not giving you a list here. Just be sensible and get an idea of what others are singing regularly.

- *Don't sing a song that you're bored with.* If you've had a song in your repertoire for ever, and you're bored with it, either take it out and put it away for a while, or reinvent it. It may have got you some great roles, and you may do it very well. But if you're bored singing it, it'll show.

The sixteen-bar song

It's unlikely in the UK, Europe or Australia that we ask you only for sixteen bars of a first song, but in America, in first and call-back rounds, it may happen. You should therefore find the best sixteen to thirty-two bars in each song. If the casting director is musical, or the musical director is present, and they happen to know the song, they might tell you the section they want to hear, but it's important that you've got several sixteen to thirty-two-bar options already prepared which show your talent off quickly. It should include your range, a money note, a belt moment, a soft moment. And of course, throughout all, have a dramatic narrative. Make sure that these bars (start and end points) are clearly indicated for the pianist. Even in the UK, Europe and Australia have these prepared as we are unlikely to hear your second song in its entirety.

What do you sing for your specific audition?

Now that you've chosen the best audition songs that should be in your general songbook, and you have all the information you need for your audition from your agent, you need to marry up the piece and the character with the songs you're going to sing for your audition. (Remember that I'm relating everything so far to your first-round audition at the moment. We're going to deal with call-backs in Chapter 5.)

The obvious choice is to *prepare songs in the style which you've been asked to sing*. When your agent was given the audition information from the casting director, you should have also been told what the panel require you to present. Don't be clever and try to do something else. If we want a jazz standard, then we want a jazz standard! Not a rock number, not a classical ballad. A jazz standard; nothing else. In the event that you've not been told specifically what to prepare, or the choice is pretty wide, then ask yourself the following questions to help you choose your songs:

The piece

Who wrote it? Do you have anything written by the composer in your portfolio already (although not from the show you are auditioning for). Remember, a composer may write in different styles, so …

What is the style of the music for this particular show? Assuming you've been able to find a recording, that should give you a real sense of the style. If you haven't been able to find out the style of the piece, then ask the casting office.

The character

If you're up for an ensemble role, then you need to consider a song that will fit the general style of the show, or focus on an understudy role that you are being asked to consider. If you're being considered for a specific part, you need to look at the general characteristics of the role. *Are they generally upbeat? Are they the underdog? Are they shy? Are they extrovert?* The list is endless. Ask yourself lots of questions. If you have been able to get a script, and read it, then you will have a good sense of the character. If you have no script, then again, get your agent to phone and ask. Choose a song that represents as many facets of your audition character as you can. You won't find an exact match, but a close approximation is better than nothing.

I have something in the style of the piece and by the same composer, but none of my songs really conveys the character I've been asked to audition for. What do I do?
The short answer is try to find a new song that is more appropriate and learn it. But I know that's not always possible and sometimes a shortage of preparation time means you can't find something new. Therefore, the long answer is *change the context of something you already have.*

Context of audition songs

Assuming you have made a good choice of portfolio songs, what I consider to be one of the most important aspects of the first-round audition song is the context in which you present it. Context relates to the setting within which your character sings the song – what has happened to them up to the point when they sing? How is your character feeling? How is your character relating to other characters? With show material (which is most likely to be given out at a call-back stage) you can be very specific about the context as it's all there in front of you. But in a first-round audition, choosing your own song, you're unlikely to have something that exactly fits the role you're auditioning for. Therefore you can either keep the original context of your chosen song (i.e. the context in which it appears in its own show, rather than the one you're auditioning for, knowing that they are similar in style) or you can change the context to better fit the role you *are* auditioning for.

This requires a lot of thought and attention to detail, but it can unleash a completely fresh approach to a song. I used to love playing around with the context of songs; it can be totally rewarding taking a song out from its original situation within a musical and giving it a brand-new context or scenario.

For example, suppose a song in its original setting relates to the character talking to their lover. What happens if, in your new context, that other person is not a lover, but their child? How does that change the delivery? Does the intention become more dramatic or urgent? Are there lyrics which are difficult to say to a child, which are easy to say to a lover, but nonetheless need to be said? By changing the person to whom your character is singing, you can reveal a whole new meaning to the song. Look at Maury Yeston's 'In A Very Unusual Way' from *Nine* in this new context, for example. It's a very different song when being sung to a child as opposed to Guido, the lover.

I'm not advocating that you always need to change the context and the changes can be very subtle, but if you do, it's best to observe the following:

- *Be sure to let the panel know why you've changed the context* – they may otherwise think you simply don't know the right version of the original or are not doing it very well, or be confused as to why you're singing that song for this audition and ask you to sing something else.

- *Be sure that you've changed the context for the right reason* – it's because you want to show an aspect of the character you are auditioning for, not just for change's sake.

- *Prepare your new context thoroughly* – don't ever go into an audition room without first having thought carefully about the changes of context you want to incorporate into your song. It's no use you thinking, 'Oh, today I'll do it like that,' because you're sure to fall flat on your face. An instinctive performance is fine, and indeed in many of my auditions and masterclasses I will play a game with auditionees and ask them to present a song within a new scenario. But in such environments, I'm acutely aware that you'll be 'winging it' for that game, and therefore make allowances. No one will make allowances for you singing a song badly or inaccurately within the audition room when you're expected to know it inside out and have prepared it thoroughly.

Should I sing a song that comes from the show I'm auditioning for in the first round of auditions?

Unless you're asked to, then no. Either choose a song from the same composer (but a different show) or from another composer of the same style.

Can I sing a song that is sung by a character of another gender, race or age?

In terms of gender, if there is a good reason why you need to, and it's a very smart choice, then I'd say yes. There are songs which come from predominantly the jazz/rock/pop categories which can be sung by both sexes, although remember to change the gender in the lyric to suit your context. In terms of age, while 'Broadway Baby' seems to be synonymous with performances by older musical theatre divas, I've heard both young girls and men sing it very successfully. So long as you give the right context and you can make it work, it's fine. Just don't sing a song as a seventy-year-old if you're only twenty-three. You have to make the new context fit your own age.

With regards to race, we have what is called colour-blind casting, meaning that an actor from any ethnicity can be considered for a role. As such, this should also mean that any song is open to interpretation by any ethnicity. However, it's generally not acceptable to sing a song outside of your ethnicity when it's obvious that the particular song refers to or has some relevance to the *character's* ethnicity. Any exceptions (and there are some – material from *Porgy and Bess, Ragtime, Once on this Island,* or *The Wiz*) may risk offending a member of the audition panel, which you want to avoid, of course. Given the obvious sensitivities surrounding racial and ethnic casting, I think that unless you have a very good reason for singing a song that goes against either your or the character's ethnicity, then don't do it.

What about accent choices within songs?

Ask where your character is from, and then choose a suitable song in that character's accent. As a general rule, sing a song with an English accent by an English composer/lyricist for an English musical. Similarly, in an American accent for a song by an American composer for an American musical. There's enough material for you to choose from without having to mix cultures and accents. The exception is when the character you're auditioning for might be European; you could easily choose any song from anywhere but with the correct European accent required.

Should I be smart, or safe with my audition song choices?

So long as you are fully prepared, you can be smart with your choices. They can be original, exciting, engaging and enlightening. But a badly prepared audition piece will let you down. Until you are confident with auditions and are confident in trying new material, I would always err on the side of safe. But 'safe' doesn't mean 'boring' – your safe song should still be energised and fresh, even though you may have sung it a hundred times. Remember, we are auditioning you, not the composer and lyricist.

I know what I want to sing, but I don't have any sheet music yet. Where do I find it?

You must never go to audition without your sheet music. Expecting the pianist to know your song by heart or intending to sing unaccompanied is not acceptable. The single exception is if you are auditioning for a production that requires actor/musicians and you are required to play an instrument. But even then, you are most likely to be expected to find something where the pianist can accompany you. There are some castings where it may be acceptable to take a CD backing (cabaret, cruise liners, etc.) but generally it's not acceptable for the professional musical theatre audition. Neither is it acceptable to present the pianist with a lyric sheet that simply contains the lyrics and chord charts or chord symbols. While the pianist will know what chords to play, they won't necessarily know the style of the accompaniment you require, and it's most likely to ruin your audition. Clear, well-marked sheet music really is the only option.

You can source sheet music from:

- libraries

- friends

- music shops

- the internet – there are many sheet music websites. Some you pay for, some you don't. Some even allow you to download your music in the appropriate musical key

- anthologies – you probably have several anthologies already, 'Audition Songs for Music Theatre' and such-like. While the anthologies can be useful, it's likely everyone else has them too so I encourage you not to be lazy; try to listen to the entire show from which an individual song comes.

Cuts

It may be that you have decided to shorten the length of your song. Remember that a song needs to be around two minutes long. For the purposes of the audition, you need to be sure that if you cut a song, it still makes dramatic sense.

Think carefully about the pianist too. They are processing information incredibly quickly to play what you require, and jumping around four pages with inaccurate signalling of cuts will result in them getting into a mess. They are your friend, so help them by being clear. Be sure to mark your music up clearly so that your pianist is absolutely certain where you need to cut from, and which bar to return to.

Also, if you make a cut to somewhere later in the song, after the cut the pianist will be expecting to stay in the same key and time signatures. If these have changed you need to make it very clear, or find a musical solution to smooth the passage between the two.

Finally, if you want the song to end earlier than it does, you may need to make a musical adjustment to the music. Adding 'end' should be fine for the pianist, but if the music suggests going into another chorus, you may need to provide a finishing chord for the pianist.

Arrangements

Generally, I would advise you to steer away from arrangements for auditions. Save them for your cabaret. Having said that, I had two fabulous arrangements I used for specific auditions. By cleverly splicing two songs together you can show off a nice range of your capabilities which an individual song might not. For example, one of mine was Sondheim's 'Not A Day Goes By' interwoven with 'Good Thing Going', both from *Merrily We Roll Along*. Providing a really great range of dramatic emotion, I loved singing it and always got a call-back with it. And of course, as with every audition song, never go into an audition with a new arrangement without being fully rehearsed on it first.

Keys

Are you sure that the song really suits you in the key it's written in? Are all the notes comfortable? Do some important notes and/or lyrics fall in the weakest part of your voice? Would you be better off having the piece in a different key? Should the piece be transposed? I did once hear an actor sing 'Love Changes Everything' from *Aspects of Love* only to drop the final dramatic note ('... same') down an octave because he couldn't sing it up top. All he needed was a transposition down a key and he'd have got it perfectly.

Transpositions

If the key in which you currently have your music is wrong, then there are several ways to get it transposed (and I mean having it transposed to paper, not transposed at sight by the pianist in the audition room on the day!)

- See if any of your musical colleagues, MDs or pianists can transpose it for you, making sure their copying is clear.

- Seek transposition services advertised in the relevant entertainment publications or magazines.

- The internet. There are several good internet transposition services (type 'Music Transposition' into your web browser). But beware that while the first transposition is normally accurate, a second transposition from the same music can create some massive errors due to the software used. If you ever have any music transposed *always* have it checked by a pianist in advance of your audition so that they can correct any accidental errors.

- Remember too that while the key may be perfect for you, it may be awful for the accompanist. Try to find a compromise that's good for both of you.

The detail in your song

Lyrics

For almost any piece, it's the lyrics that will instantly guide you to a good performance. Remember, musical theatre is about *acting*, not just singing or dancing, and so the words your character sings or the acting intention behind your steps, are vitally important.

- For the moment, try to separate yourself from the tune. Just concentrate on the lyrics.

- I used to find it very useful to write the lyrics out, omitting all the punctuation, and keeping them in full sentences rather than writing them in verse layout as in a poem. I then used to highlight the nouns, the repetition of words, metaphors, and other poetical elements and devices the lyricist has used to convey the meaning and emotion of the song. Why did the lyricist use that particular word? Why was that noun stronger than another? Does the character really mean what is being sung? Why does the lyric repeat: to stress the point, or to question what is said? Does the character need assurance?

- Questions to ask yourself (regardless of whether it's the original context or your own):

   Is the character singing alone (as in a soliloquy) and the thoughts are internal, or are they singing to someone?

If to someone, who is it? What is the character's relationship to the other person?

What does your character want to convey to that person? What's the purpose?

Do they actually say what they mean, or do they skirt around the edges?

What mood is your character employing to get the point across? Anger, frustration, sympathy, flirtatiousness?

- Remember that lyrics are not meant to be read, they're meant to be sung. So you must give due consideration to their presentation in the same way that you would dialogue. Of course, unlike dialogue, they have a fixed rhythm to the musical melody as dictated by the composer, but that doesn't mean they shouldn't be treated with the utmost thought and attention. Diction, weight (which words have more emphasis than others), breathing, phrasing, pacing, intention – all these aspects need to be thought out carefully and choices made.

For all this detailed work, don't get too bogged down by having to find the 'perfect' choice – that's what rehearsal is for. You do, however, need to make a 'good' choice. Just singing the song with no thought whatsoever will be dull. You need to be very clear about why your character is singing this song and what your character's dramatic intention is throughout the song (or the dance). There will be many options – choose the one you think works best.

Music

- Once you've put the lyrics back together and have a

better understanding of them and, more importantly, have made certain dramatic choices as to what the lyrics say about the emotions of the character, then you can study the music.

- Look at the structure of the song – both musically and lyrically – and ask yourself: does it have a structure of verse-chorus-verse-chorus with a key change and a final chorus? Or is it more irregular? What does the structure therefore say about the character? Decisive? Thoughtful? Scatty? Irreverent? Scared? Lonely?

- It doesn't really matter whether you read music or not, although I would certainly advise anyone serious about a career in musical theatre to consider learning simple music theory and how to read a single line of music. There are any number of one-day courses available, and if you can't find them via the internet, why not ask a musical director or rehearsal pianist to spend a couple of hours teaching you the basics? Most musicians are more than happy to help and encourage you, and normally a bottle of wine and a sandwich lunch will be sufficient payment if you're nice. You really ought to be able to recognise simple elements from the music: where the tune gets higher or lower, louder and softer, which notes need attack, which notes are sustained. Each of these basic elements relates directly to the composer's intentions of what the character's emotions are, and while you may wish to question and then change them if you have adopted a new context, you must at least be knowledgeable about what you're changing; what the original intentions were. Assuming the writing partnership is a good one, the lyricist and the composer will have taken a great amount of time to ensure that the two elements (melody and lyric) complement each other perfectly and make a coherent whole.

- How do the melody and the lyric work together? Where does the melody take the lyric? Does a rising melody support a rise in tension of the lyric? Or are they purposely at odds with each other? Does the lyric reflect a change in the melody? What do your answers to these questions say about the character's emotional state?

Accompaniment

Once you've looked at the vocal melody line, have a look at the accompaniment and see what the piano plays underneath your vocal line. Is the accompaniment big and dramatic, or simple and quiet? Are there melodies from other songs which might suggest a dramatic connection with this song? Is the accompaniment dramatically in harmony with your character or is it purposely in conflict? There may be further musical clues to help you with character.

Rehearsing your song

Preparation, preparation and preparation. Remember? You have to work through and know all your songs thoroughly before you use them in an audition scenario. Half of your preparation work will already have been done through the advice given in the previous sections, but now it's necessary to pull all your ideas together and form your performance.

- *The song as a whole*: Work out what your character's emotional journey is throughout the song. And what effect does that have on the delivery of the song? Does it start out quiet and grow to deliver a big finish? Does it have a climax in the middle of the song?

- *The initial phrase*: What does that first sentence say and how are you going to grab us? This initial phrase is vitally important in setting the mood and tone of your song, and capturing our attention. A phrase is not just a series of notes, any more than a sentence is a series of words. When the notes and words combine, they create a whole (the phrase or the sentence), which in its entirety should be satisfying and captivating and make a point.

- *General phrasing*: How are you going to phrase your sentences throughout the song? What is the musical shape of individual phrases? How do phrases build the emotion of your song?

- *The last phrase*: Your final phrase is as important as the first and is the lasting impression you give us – if it's a big ending, it needs to be solid and secure. If it's a quiet ending, it still needs to have an energy and intensity that draws us in further still.

- *Last phrase vowels*. Don't change a vowel sound when it falls on a difficult or sustained high note. One particular culprit is the 'ee' vowel (as in knee), which far too many singers try to compensate by singing 'i-ee' (as in 'eye'), clicking in an 'ee' sound at the very last second. Don't cheat. Work on your 'ee' vowels throughout your range.

- *Breathing*: You are likely to be either nervous or excited on the day, and the second thing to let you down will be your breathing (the first is normally the shakes). It's therefore really important that you know where and how you're going to breathe throughout your song. Again, working with a vocal coach on your material will sort this out in more detail but key points about where to breathe are:

Look at the lyrics to give you the best clue and use the punctuation as good breathing places.

Try not to breathe mid-sentence, unless it's a very long, slow phrase.

Try not to breathe before the important end words of a sentence. The lyricist will almost certainly be placing key/strong words at the end of the sentence so we need to hear them.

Try experimenting with *not* taking a breath – it can be very effective to 'ride' a beautiful melody without taking a breath at an obvious place. It means that you may need to grab a sneaky top-up breath; try not to make it too obvious.

Make sure you have enough breath to finish your phrase, and particularly to finish your song. There's nothing more disappointing than someone singing a song really well only to spoil the ending by not having breathed properly so that the 'money' note dies away before it should.

- *Vocal tone and quality*: Each style of music requires a change of vocal quality and tone, of course. But even within a song, you should experiment with where you can show different qualities of tone colour within your phrases. Varying the sound of your voice can portray very different emotions and intensity. Use the lyrics to guide you as to which effects to employ.

- *Rhythm* – Be conscious of the rhythm. As a general rule, sing the notes exactly as they are written, giving each note its full length. The exception to this is pop or jazz writing, where you can be freer in your interpretation. Never 'back-phrase' (hold back or stretch the melody) for songs within the Golden Age period or before unless you are doing a specific new arrangement.

- *Pace and speed* – Be aware that in an audition, your sense of speed will be running a little faster due to excitement, so be cautious and go for a slightly slower tempo – in the audition room, you'll be about right. Rushing through a song can ruin it. Plan to take your time and allow the music to breathe. Find the sections where you can change the pace by becoming quicker or slowing down. Be sure to mark this in your music for the pianist.

- *Diction*: Carefully practise your diction, particularly if you are singing in an accent. We must be able to understand the words in every scenario – if we can't hear every syllable you may as well be humming. Endings of words should be crisp and clean, particularly 'd's and 't's.

- *Dynamics*: The louds and softs of music. Although I'm a fairly competent and instinctive musician, in practice I often found it useful to visualise in my head the dynamics when I was working on a song. It helped give a real sense of shape to the phrase I was singing. You must know where each phrase starts and how it grows dynamically as a result of (or as a cause of) your melodic and lyrical emotions. But beware not to start your song too softly. You want the audition panel to be captured at the start, not straining to hear you. Conversely, I recently had an audition where a woman sang 'The Sound of Music' and after a beautifully delicate, quiet introduction started her phrase like a foghorn. I asked whether she'd intended to frighten all the goats off the mountain.

- Use gradual changes of dynamics and articulation throughout your piece to build tension, surprise, variation and drama.

- *Accents*: If you are required to sing in an accent, be sure that you have worked on the whole song in the accent. An accent may considerably change the way in which you sing the song, both technically and emotionally. And be sure to maintain the accent throughout. If the accent has a particularly obscure vowel sound on a particular note, you can't change it for an easier vowel. Bizarrely, in the UK, I do find actors aiming to sing with an English accent slipping into American accents. Either they've heard it sung that way, or they simply can't hear themselves.

I could go into significantly more detail, but given everyone's individuality, I hope these elements help focus on the musical aspects of your song.

Vocal delivery – lessons and classes

In terms of the technical vocal delivery of your song, I'm afraid I'm not a voice coach and it would therefore be wrong of me to advise you how to sing a song technically. Also, with the huge variety of songs available to you to audition with, it would be impossible to deconstruct a specific song with you here, as every song is unique in its own way.

Interpretation and delivery are vitally important, however, and as well as working on your own, you must seek every opportunity to take classes in both voice production and technique with a vocal teacher. Tuition costs money, I know, but this is all part of the preparation I keep talking about. What is the point of spending hours working on the background to your material and knowing how you want to deliver the song dramatically if your voice lets you down by being technically inadequate? In the same breath, you may have the most astoundingly good technical voice, but if you don't know how to interpret a song, you're 'just a good voice' and not much use to the production.

Finding a good vocal teacher is similar to finding a good agent: someone you trust, can work with, and with whom you can develop a relationship. Someone who is sympathetic to your musical needs. Someone who will challenge you. Someone who will stretch you. You should ask around for a good tutor; friends, musical directors and agents will all have useful contacts.

Also try to record the accompaniment at lessons to aid your private rehearsals. While it does mean that you're restricted to the 'set' tempo of the recording, if you want to change the overall tempo, or want to play around a little with the arrangement by making cuts, it's far better to suffer this rather than singing with nothing at all.

Sing through your song in its entirety

Whether you hire a pianist, rehearse with a vocal coach or work on your own, you must go through the entire song several times. You have to know what physical and technical aspects you require to sing the whole song through, pacing yourself and getting a sense of the entire piece. I know many actors (and one of them was me) who either worked on the song in sections, or never sang the song with the same volume and intensity of an audition situation. Consequently I didn't fully understand the support and technical ability required to sing the song in its entirety. Singers are sometimes worn out by the end of the piece because they pushed too hard at the beginning of the song. They'd have known not to if they had worked properly on the full song in advance.

Preparing your sheet music

Having worked on your song and determined how you intend to sing it, you now need to mark your music so that your pianist will know what your intentions are.

- Using a yellow highlighter and a ruler, carefully highlight the key signature, the time signature, repeat signs, multiple endings, codas and any dynamic markings.

- If you have decided to cut a song, mark the music very clearly with a large box in black felt tip, and a large cross within it.

- If you want to make speed changes that are not already in the music, add them clearly. You don't need to use posh Italian musical terminology. 'Slower' or 'faster' will be perfectly acceptable.

- If you have added a pause, or require a break in the music, make large vertical double lines in the music.

- If you want to start or finish in a different place from that suggested in the music, you need to add 'START HERE' or 'FINISH HERE' with an arrow facing downwards.

- Consider whether you need to hear the tune in the piano part. Some vocal score arrangements have the tune in the accompaniment, and it isn't always necessary for the pianist to play it. If you don't want it, write 'TUNE NOT REQUIRED' at the beginning of your music.

- Keep your markings clean and succinct. A messy, unclear mark-up of your music won't help your friend the pianist, and inevitably will have a major impact on your audition.

Taping your sheet music together

Since you don't know what type of music stand your pianist has, it's far better to let the pianist decide how he wants to fold the music, rather than you. Therefore, the simplest way to tape your music is to lay your pages flat in page order with the music facing you, and simply tape 1 to 2, 2 to 3, 3 to 4, etc. down the long side. When you place them in your music folder, you can 'concertina-fold' the music. This way the pianist can either play from the music in a 'book' fold, or unfold the music completely so all of the pages are visible. The pianist can also control difficult page turns this way.

Also be aware of the tape you use. Use a non-shiny tape – shiny tape over notes can cause glare and the pianist may not be able to see clearly. A matte tape doesn't produce glare, and indeed is almost transparent.

Organising your portfolio

Having spoken to many audition pianists, the consensus seems to be that music within bound plastic wallet folders is *not* the most helpful binding. The glare of the plastic can often hinder sight-reading as strong theatre lights reflect off the glossy page, and the heavy binding to ensure that the plastic sheets stay together often makes page-turning difficult. So most pianists prefer reading music copied on to white matte paper.

Given the fact that you will need to take several pieces of music to your audition, you still need a waterproof carrier to cart around your auditions. This is where the plastic folders can be helpful, but take them out from the sleeves for the pianist. I also used to have each style of song colour-coded with the title of the song, but that's my stationery fetish kicking in.

Remember that your binder needn't necessarily house *all* your music collection – keep a box at home for that – and just take the binder containing the songs that are appropriate for the style of audition you're attending. I had several binders which contained songs for each style of music, resulting in my having to take only one fairly slim binder to auditions, instead of an entire heavy collection of songs, 90 per cent of which I didn't need for that specific audition. However, always take one or two songs outside of the style which show range just in case someone wants to hear something else.

Also add an index page at the front – if a musical director wants to hear something else from you, it's quicker to show him an A4 page with all your songs on for him to choose. Too much time is wasted in an audition flicking through pages trying to find a song.

Finally, some general points about your portfolio.

- Having taken all this trouble to put your songs together, make sure you know what's in there. Have a look through it regularly and scan the lyrics. Read them before you go to bed. When you're cooking have a sing to yourself, or in the shower. Anywhere, any time, have a sing of some of the songs just to reinforce them in your brain.

- If there's something in there that you aren't 150 per cent confident with, it shouldn't be there. Chances are that if a musical director flicks through your folder in the audition room, they will pick the one you haven't done in years … (in which case be honest and ask if you can stand around the piano so you can see the words).

- As you become more experienced, change your repertoire. On a rainy day, get the whole lot out, and ask yourself which songs are tired and lifeless, which you are bored with and which keep getting you rejected. Get rid of them and put some new life into your audition material.

- If copies are beginning to look a bit rough with scratches or tear marks, get a new copy made from your original.

But don't forget to write in all your markings for the pianist again.

- Be sure you know *why* your song is in your portfolio, and if you come across a new song that shows you off better, replace the old one.

- Take the copy, not the original. I would strongly advise you always to keep your original music at home and take photocopies into the audition. I once lost my entire portfolio of original songs on a train while I was auditioning on tour. I never saw it again and it took ages to rebuild my audition book, particularly as some of the songs had been rare.

When you copy your music, bear the following in mind:

- Make sure the copy is clear and readable, with no smudges or marks.

- Copy on to white matte paper of a fairly heavy weight. Light card is best, but your copyist will advise you. Paper weight of over 180gsm works best.

- Copy single-sided only.

- Be sure that everything is visible and nothing has been clipped off the edges. Some music scores are odd shapes, in which case you may need to reduce the music slightly on the copy machine to fit everything on. Again, your copyist should be able to do this for you. But don't make the music too small either, leaving huge white margins around the page. The pianist must be able to read it clearly.

- Be particularly careful that the left-hand side of the page is clear and not fuzzy or deleted. For the pianist, the left-hand side of the music has vital information, including the time signature, the key signature and the clef.

• If the title doesn't fit, then write it on afterwards.

If you take care of your song portfolio, it will serve you well for your entire career, and you will always be presenting yourself as a professional, conscientious and employable performer.

Spoken monologues and acting scenes

While it's becoming less likely that you'll need a monologue for your musical theatre audition (as you will normally be given text directly from the production in your call-back), it's always best to have a few speeches up your sleeve. We will look at how to prepare spoken text in Chapter 5 – 'The Call-back'.

Since it's rare for you to need one, the following advice should suffice for the purposes of the musical theatre audition:

• As with the choosing of musical theatre songs, your monologue must come from the different genres of theatre, although not necessarily from musical theatre. Avoid, however, anything from television or film for a musical theatre audition – keep to stage texts.

• If you are asked to prepare a monologue, look back at the tips I gave you above in relation to choosing your song. The monologue should try to encapsulate as many of those elements as possible, such as whether it's suitable for the character, appropriate to the genre and period of the production, etc.

- Try to vary the styles of your monologue. In the same way as we looked at different genres of musical theatre writing, you should aim to have a good monologue from each of the following categories (again, this is a broad sweep of authors – find those others who you enjoy):

  something from Shakespeare

  something from either Ibsen, Chekhov, Arthur Miller, Eugene O'Neill or Tennessee Williams

  something considered classically 'modern': Michael Frayn, Neil Simon, Tom Stoppard, Harold Pinter, Brian Friel, Simon Gray, David Mamet, Terence McNally, Tony Kushner, Kenneth Lonergan or Richard Greenberg

  something current and possibly edgy: Mark Ravenhill, Joe Orton, Neil LaBute, Leo Butler, Jez Butterworth, Lucy Prebble

- Often, for audition purposes only, 'new' monologues can be created from duologues where the other role is cut. You have to be sure that without the other spoken role the monologue still makes sense, but such an exercise means that your character is speaking to someone and with an objective, rather than being an internal monologue.

- As with your songs, it's not enough just to know your monologue – you need to know the whole piece and certainly the scene from which your monologue comes. If you can see a production of the play, great. If not, you have to read the whole play.

- If you have been given your audition at very short notice, and you don't have any monologue ready, as a very last resort consider speaking the lyrics of a suitable song. Such an exercise will probably work better with more modern pieces than period pieces, and you will need to choose very carefully as not all songs will work. Some tips are:

Try your hardest to break the musical rhythm of the melody if you speak the lyric. Try not to make the lyric sound like a poem and really aim for making the sentences sound like sentences instead of musical phrases.

Try not to emphasise a rhyme.

Take your time between sentences. Without any musicality or rhythm to adhere to, you can give new pauses, new intentions, new pace and new irony to what is now a speech as opposed to a sung lyric.

Don't choose an overly dramatic song – it'll probably seem a bit naff as a speech.

Try it now – have a look at the lyrics of *Cabaret*, or 'Bill's Soliloquy' from *Carousel*, or 'Movie in My Mind' from *Miss Saigon*. It's an excellent exercise for you to do anyway, regardless of whether you end up using it as a monologue or not.

Don't neglect the plethora of good musical theatre scene-work, much of which was crafted by playwrights.

Once you have a couple of monologues, type them out and put them in the back of your song portfolio, regularly running over them ready for the odd occasion when you'll need one.

Auditioning while on tour

It's very likely that you will be asked to audition while you're on tour, and if so, you must still be prepared. While the audition panel are likely to be a little more tolerant of your choice of song if we know you are away from home and don't have your full portfolio, it will not do you any favours if you come into the audition with one inappropriate song and nothing else. Therefore, keep a slimmed-down version of your song portfolio with you when you tour. It still needs to have contrasting songs, but instead of a wide range, you can limit what you take.

Remember, too, that your touring colleagues will also have songs with them. You may not have brought something appropriate, but they may have something in their portfolio that you can borrow. However, be sure that it's in your key, and if they have specific markings on their music which relate to their performance and which you don't want to do, you need to mask them somehow. Ideally, copy the music again, and mark out what you don't need. Be sure not to tamper with their original – that's sure to ruin a friendship and you certainly don't want that on tour.

Musical directors may be generous in giving time to work on a song with you when you're on tour. They may say no, of course, but if you've built up a good relationship with them over the course of the tour, they will probably be more than happy to help you.

As with your music, you'll also need your dance shoes and appropriate audition clothing in your suitcase.

You should also make sure that your agent tells the casting office you're not currently based at home. Travel can be extraordinarily expensive, and a casting director may well be helpful in limiting the number of auditions we ask you to attend. I have sometimes waited to bring touring actors in at the later audition rounds in order to reduce the number of auditions they need to attend. We can't always be so considerate, but at least this can be discussed with the audition panel if we know.

When you take your appointment details from your agent, make sure you can actually get to the audition in time, and also get back to perform in the evening. Most casting directors will be sympathetic towards someone on tour, and will be grateful for you having made the effort of a four-hour train journey. So it's OK to say that you must be out of the audition room by 4.20 as you need to catch a train back to your touring venue. Similarly, if the auditions are running late, tell the registrar or the casting director as soon as possible so you can get away in time.

Also tell the company manager of the production you are touring with. Should there be an emergency on tour, such as a sick actor, they'll need to know where you are, and how long it'll take you to get back. And finally, don't lie in order to make an audition. I have known actors claim to be sick from a production, only to go to the airport or station, do an amazing audition and then miraculously recover for their next performance. You will get found out and I won't cover for you.

Keeping physically and mentally 'match fit'

I haven't forgotten about dancers! But in terms of dance auditioning, however, it's difficult to 'prepare' anything specific for dance auditions in advance because you will be taught the dance routine in the room when you audition, which we'll explore in Chapter 4.

However, you absolutely must keep your body in good shape in between auditions and jobs. If you are a serious dancer, that means attending a range of classes in order to keep yourself in peak condition. Even if you're not a great dancer, you certainly won't improve by sitting about all day. Get out, go to classes, get fit, stretch, do coordination exercises – anything that will help you for when the call comes telling you that a dance audition is imminent.

For those of you auditioning while you are currently in heavily dance-based shows, you will probably be in pretty good shape already given that you're dancing eight times a week. There's a term I use relating to such artists – 'match fit' – by which I mean they are energised, alive, confident, ready to work, on the ball. They exude a vibe that says 'I'm ready – cast me.'

If you haven't performed for a while, you may have let yourself go a bit. Your dancing and singing may have become a bit rusty and, in your day job, you may be sitting down 90 per cent of the day, doing little exercise and eating poorly. You hate your job, you're not getting auditions and you're losing confidence. You're disheartened, and very quickly you get in a downward spiral of negative feelings. As a result, you're desperate – your landlord is threatening to kick you out and you can't understand why your best mate (who is just as talented as you) has just got a great role in the latest hot musical.

As inevitable as it is when things don't quite go according to plan, keep negativity away by maintaining your skills, keeping alive and committed.

- Take singing and dancing classes, or if you can't afford them, ensure you stretch and exercise at home or at the gym. Buy vocal warm-up CDs and go through them at least twice a week. Put on your show CDs and sing along. It doesn't matter if you have them in your song portfolio or not; the fact is you're singing and giving yourself a vocal workout.

- Teach – that's a great way of keeping you on the ball.

And most drama colleges value professionals on their part-time staff.

- Keep working on your songs and monologue material, reminding yourself that the more you work on them, the more you are likely to be confident with them and the better the chances are that you'll get a job.

- Go to the theatre as often as you can so that you keep acquainted with what's on. There are very often discounts on tickets for actors' union members or under-26s, most cities have 'half price' theatre outlets, and many shows will do discounts on tickets bought on the day. You could also join theatre discount clubs which get group discounts, or 'showbiz' websites which have special offers. And most times you can get a sense of the show from the cheaper seats without having to starve for a week. If you can't afford to go to the theatre, watch TV, but not just for fun; be critical of how performers are acting and what you think of them.

- Write a diary, write songs, write stories, write limericks, draw, make jewellery, be *creative* – keep your imagination active and alive. Soak up everything aesthetic that you can; read, write, watch and learn.

- Make a commitment to looking good.

- Eat well and healthily, and drink plenty of water.

- Avoid people who are negative all the time, or consistently talk about how well *they're* doing. Such people will make you feel considerably worse. If you are struggling to find work, you want to be with people who enlighten, encourage, energise, help and inspire you.

- And most important of all …

> **Remain positive at all times. It's often hard in this difficult business, but being positive is one of the most important personality traits for any performer. Many will try to put you down – you shouldn't be one of them.**

And with all that in the forefront of your mind, let's get on with the audition.

WORDS OF WISDOM

Research

Vanessa Scammell

I have discovered that one of the most common shortcomings encountered in the auditioning process is the failure to research the show for which the audition is being held. As a musical director I am constantly amazed at how little the artist knows about the piece. Research the work. Who was the composer? Find the most recognised songs from the piece and indeed which character sings them. This will help you determine which role or roles would suit you best. Now, if the panel feels you 'fit' a particular role, you may be required to sing a few bars of one or more of the show's popular pieces in the first stage of the audition as a simple vocal range exercise. Having familiarised yourself with those 'most recognised' or 'popular' songs prior to walking into that room and therefore executing them proficiently, you significantly enhance the possibility of a call-back. Give yourself the best possible advantage. A little homework can prove invaluable.

Preparation

David Gilmore

Be *thoroughly* prepared! You need to sit confidently on top of the material, not let it sit on top of *you*. Nerves arise from a fear of what can go wrong. Leave nothing to chance. You don't have to overdo it, but allowing the dead hand of audition nerves to so dampen your natural vivacity that you appear dull or 'glum' can be offputting. You have to welcome your nerves, learn how to turn them to advantage, utilise them as an extra source of stimulating energy, sharpening your abilities and giving you an 'edge' that brightens and polishes your performance.

Gareth Valentine

Preparation is everything in an audition. Over many years of taking them, I am still surprised at the lack of preparation and readiness in the UK compared to what one finds across the pond in America.

Your songs, speeches, tap shoes, dancing clothes are the tools of your trade – choose them well and keep them in good condition. I have known time and again people turn up to auditions without music or without knowing a learned monologue or speech. Next time a plumber turns up to do a job at their home without tools, what right have they to complain?! Have a folio deep-filled with diverse material all hardwired in the memory. If you have to prepare new material, find a professional coach to guide you through it – it could mean the difference between success and failure.

Asking questions and making choices

Jamie Lloyd

If it is a requirement of the role, you must sing well (and in the appropriate style) for the musical director and you will have to dance to the choreographer's exacting standards, but for me it is all about the acting. It is all very well being able to hit the 'money notes' or kick your legs up to your ears, but unless you've made decisions as to why you're singing that lyric or launching into that split leap, it is all redundant. Your first job is to be a storyteller. What is the intention of the dance? What is the context of that audition song you've selected? Who are you singing to? Do you know the show it is from or are you inventing a new scenario? When you're preparing for the meeting, first speak your song as a monologue, connecting to the truth of what you're saying. Add the notes after, retaining the connection to the narrative. If you've been given an extract to read, try to get hold of the full text. If the text leads into a song, think about why that happens. Remember the old musical theatre adage: when the stakes are so high and the passion is so great that the spoken word is no longer enough to express what you're thinking or feeling, you sing; when singing is no longer enough, you dance.

The audition pieces

Vanessa Scammell

One of the most important aspects of any audition is how you present yourself. Obviously. Certainly in musical theatre, how you present your song really matters. Singing along to a recording is vastly different to the 'nakedness' of singing solely with piano accompaniment. So, get with a pianist! Also, apart from your prepared work, always have a contrasting piece in your repertoire as an alternative. Often the panel will want to see if another vocal approach or style may be better suited to you. And if so, this may present more possibilities for you in the broader sense of the show's casting. And make sure you present the audition pianist with well printed-out music. This means legible lyrics, the correct key and clear markings for cuts and repeats. If you need the piece transposed, engage a professional to do it, or at least to check it over. One of my highlights as an audition pianist was being presented with a screwed-up piece of paper from an auditionee's pocket with three chords written on it. Needless to say they didn't go through to the next round.

David Gilmore

Always have plenty of choice on offer: a whole range of thoroughly prepared material in different musical styles, different tempi, and from differing eras. You and the auditioner can select something suited to the show and the part, and then be able to do something completely contrasting if necessary. Sheet music should be in the correct key.

SECTION TWO

THE AUDITION

3

THE DAY OF YOUR AUDITION

'I Feel Witty' blares out as your mobile ringtone goes off, waking you from a deep sleep.

'Mmmm?' you just about manage to muster, having found your phone from within the folds of your duvet.

'Hello, darling. Bad moment? It's Dorothy, dear. Just had a call from the audition rooms.' A pause. 'Darling?' Another pause. 'Sweetie, *where are you*!?'

After several expletives you look at the clock: 11.56. Your audition was half an hour ago.

'Dorothy! Oh, Dorothy …' and several expletives later, you throw your alarm clock at the wall.

'All right, all right. Calm down, sweetie. I'll tell them you're stuck in traffic. Be there at 2.30. And darling … never again!'

So, just when you thought you were going to have an early night, you decided that it was better to go to the first-night party of *Legally Hairsprayed* the night before and invite the more attractive members of the ensemble back to your home for a naughty game of 'Hide the Mic Pack' until 4 a.m. Bad move.

Now, I like a good party too. But please, if you know you've got an audition the next day, do be sensible. There'll be many occasions when you can stay out until the early hours, but the night before an audition is not one of them.

The night before

Instead of that party, get to bed early and before you drift off, just have another look at the songs you've chosen to sing. Go over the words, think about what they mean, and reinforce the intentions and choices that you've given them. There have been studies on athletes who claim to have improved their performance significantly by simply 'imagining' their event. They remain completely still, yet positively imagining the event in their mind seems to have a positive effect on the real outcome. So, do the same. Imagine yourself happy and assured, entering the room, greeting the panel, singing your song wonderfully (and actually go through the song in your head, line by line as if your were performing it) and leaving the room brimming with confidence and energy.

Sounds daft, huh? I don't know why it should work but if nothing else, it gives you a positive feeling to go to sleep with, and one which will, ideally, remain when you get up.

Oh, and remember to set your alarm.

Illness

I've woken up and feel absolutely awful, have tried to warm up and cannot sing a note. Nothing's coming out. I really ought to go back to bed.

Despite our good intentions of aiming to keep in prime condition, the simple fact is that everyone gets sick now and then. And you will feel considerably worse auditioning when you know you're not doing your best. It's at this point that you must decide whether you really can or can't attend the audition. But:

- Remember that there were several thousand people

who were submitted but who haven't got an audition. By pulling out, it means someone else is missing an opportunity, as we are unlikely to be able to fill your audition slot at the last minute.

- Remember that you have been specially chosen to show us how brilliant you are.

- Remember that this audition is a fantastic opportunity for you.

I'm saying this not to make you feel guilty, but to make you question just how sick you are. So if you have a niggle in your throat and just need another ten minutes' warm-up, then do it.

If you really are sick, then phone your agent at the earliest opportunity, and he will then call the casting office. It's very important for the casting director to know that you're not well. There are two things likely to happen.

- We'll either try to rearrange your audition for another day, and hope you've recovered.

- Or we'll explain that this is the only day, and even if you're under par, it's better we see you and make allowances than not see you at all. You then need to ascertain how serious your illness is and whether you can do enough to get you through to the next round.

I'm generally reluctant to call someone in who is sick and will always try to change the audition if I can. I also worry about the damage someone can potentially do to their voice if it's already in a bad state. The most disappointing situation is that we may simply not be able to fit you in another day or you may not recover until after the final auditions. Sadly that'll be the end of the road ... this time.

If you do struggle in, be absolutely sure that your agent has told us in advance that you're at death's door. But once you're in the audition room try not to make excuses. If you've made sure we know you're not 100 per cent in advance, just do your very best. We will make allowances. Concentrate on being the best you can.

For dance auditions, obviously if you have an injury that could be worsened by doing the audition, then please don't attend and risk further damage.

A word of warning. If you are *not* sick, and you happen to crack on a note, or can't reach a high phrase, don't use the excuse afterwards of 'Oh, I think I've got laryngitis' or some other naughty fib. Real sickness is excusable, but simply lying because you didn't warm up properly is not. And when you see as many people as we do, day in day out, we know pretty quickly who the deceivers are!

Check the travel report

Check that your mode of transport has no delays. Bearing in mind you need to be at your audition fifteen minutes before your call time (possibly more if it's a dance audition, to enable you to warm up properly), that fifteen minutes can easily be eaten up by a cancelled train or heavy traffic. Of course, you can do little about such problems, but if you know in advance you can at least leave earlier. If you're not going to make your appointment time, call your agent or the casting office to tell them you'll be late.

Warming up

If you're going to your audition from home, then please make time to warm up thoroughly. You will definitely benefit. I'm always staggered at how few actors warm up prior to auditions, only to then come in and wonder why they can't sing or move properly.

And I don't mean just vocally warming up.

There's an actor friend of mine who is fastidious about his yoga regime; he goes to class devotedly for several hours every morning at 5.30 a.m. and while I think he's completely insane, he is energised, mentally alert and physically warmed up for his day ahead. Furthermore, he's one of the few actors I can call in for a 10 a.m. audition who's 'on the money' first thing.

Now while many would be daunted by his strict regime (and I'm certainly in awe of him), his dedication is hugely impressive and rewarding. It peeves me when we get requests from actors who can't take morning meetings because they *'don't sound as good'*. Get up early and warm up!

Before you leave for the audition, start with a vocal warm-up. Purchase an exercise tape, or record exercises from your lessons.

- Start quietly with simple breathing exercises.

- Then gentle humming, leading to vowel exercises on scales and arpeggios.

- Gentle slides on different intervals, and then bit by bit increase your volume, range, speed and flexibility so that your whole voice begins to 'kick in'.

- Take your specific exercises and work your voice in. Don't go to your high notes too soon; get there over the range of your exercises so that you're fully warmed up.

- Don't forget the tongue twisters and staccato exercises.

- Pick out the more difficult phrases in your songs, or those with difficult intonation and jumps. Be sure they're firmly placed in your mind.

- Finally, sing your songs in their entirety. Ideally you should be able to sing them full out, but don't work so hard in the warm-up so that you'll be tired for the audition. The aim is to warm yourself up, not wear yourself out!

Physical exercise, for a music or acting audition, can be fairly simple. It's really about stretching and getting your blood flowing. Some bends, some reaches, some head rolls. Keep it simple, relaxed and focused. This isn't a gym workout, just a bit of a wake-up for your body.

Of course, for a dance audition you will be expected to arrive before the dance call time in order to give yourself a proper warm-up and stretch in the room.

Mental preparation is also important, and from the minute you step out of your house, if not before, you should aim to be in a positive, energised mental state right up until the point where you've finished your audition. Try to keep focused, and not get distracted. Keep alert. Visualise your audition again. You feel great waiting to go in, you look fabulous, your name is called out and you step up to the door excited at being given this terrific opportunity. You stand in the centre singing brilliantly with focus and attentiveness to detail. Your audition is wonderful, you are joyous, the team are thrilled and you leave the room happy, relaxed and in control of everything.

Clothing and hair

Dress
So many people ask whether they should dress in the style of the character or not. I tend to lean towards the rule of:

> **Unless you've been asked by the casting office to wear something specific, then go neutral and plain, with a sensible and subtle nod towards the period of the piece.**

When we were casting *Guys and Dolls* for London, we asked all the men to audition in a suit; a man's posture really changes when he wears a jacket and trousers as opposed to jeans and a T-shirt. Similarly for *La Cage aux Folles* we asked the Cagelle auditionees to wear something that showed off their legs and physique, and – if they had them – to wear heels. With *Rent* we asked people to come in with a hint of 'street' wear – something a bit funky.

You don't need to go to extreme lengths to dress the role. We have costume designers to do that. But visual perceptions are important, so unless a costume requirement is specifically asked for, then for singing and acting auditions, ask yourself what the period is, and then consider something from your wardrobe which complements the period style and character.

If you're unsure of the period, and you can't find out, general rules are:

- Men: a nice plain open-necked shirt (no loud patterns) and a pair of smart trousers with smart shoes.

- Women: a skirt and complementing top with heels. If it's a more modern piece, then trousers are OK if you feel it's appropriate to the character. Depending on the period, a long-ish skirt might be appropriate.

- Jeans should *only* be worn if it's a modern piece and you think they add a certain flavour to the character. If you're not sure, don't wear them.

- Keep colours neutral – black is always a safe bet although a little boring, but if your character is comic or a lighter character, go brighter (not fluorescent – just brighter!).

- Good shoes – no trainers. I have worked with a director who has a real thing about shoes, equating how good the performer will be with the quality of their footwear. He didn't always get it right, but it worked in his favour more times than not ...

- If your physique is fit and defined, then wear something fitted that shows it off. If you've missed a few sessions at the gym, then wear something that complements your shape.

- No logos or messages. (I did have someone once wear a sweatshirt which shouted in pink fluorescent letters 'HIRE ME!'... I didn't.)

- No coloured lucky socks. If you've prepared properly, trust me, you can leave them at home.

Remember that this is, after all, a job interview. OK, not a job interview for a position in, say, a bank, where a certain formality is required, but an interview nonetheless. So someone well presented, clean and smart says to the panel, '*I want to look good for you, I want to work hard for you, I'm prepared to put the work in, I'm prepared to make the effort.*'

You might decide to use your clothes to help a dramatic emotional moment in your song – it could be that the tugging of a sleeve, or removing a jacket or jumper adds something physically dramatic and poignant. Planning a little subtle costume 'drama' can be interesting and shows you've thought about the piece.

Dance wear

On the whole, what to wear for dance auditions is much less about 'smartness' than it is about wearing appropriate clothing which a) allows us to ascertain that you have the technical capabilities that are required and b) allows us to see your physicality. Therefore make sure that:

- your clothes don't restrict your movement

- your clothes show off your physique and as much of your body as is respectful (Oh, have I seen some sights in a dance studio at 9.30 in the morning!)

- your clothes aren't 'flowing' so that your movements seem blurred when you dance

- your clothes aren't too long for you so that you risk tripping

Men would normally wear some form of dance support or jockstrap, and girls might consider a support/running bra. Additionally, girls should have a practice skirt and boys should have a pair of kneepads.

Dance shoes

If you're a serious dancer, then men should invest in a pair of good-quality split-sole jazz trainers, flat jazz shoes and tap shoes, and women should also have split-sole jazz trainers, plus heeled dance shoes (known as 'New Yorkers'), flat jazz shoes, tap shoes and ballet/pointe shoes. Obviously the best quality you can afford ensures a longer life and better support, and do regularly check straps or laces for fraying, and make sure heels and taps are secure. I've witnessed several nasty injuries during dance auditions where a heel has broken and someone has fallen. Similarly, taps coming off (and flying towards the panel) is dangerous. And while you can of course borrow some shoes if something breaks, a change in size, or your feet feeling odd in another's shoes, can ruin your audition.

If you're not a prime dancer, then as a minimum you should invest in some jazz trainers, or regular trainers that give your feet some flexibility, and some kneepads. Female dancers should also invest in some dance shoes with a little bit of heel.

Hair

- Whatever your normal hairstyle, try your best to keep your hair appropriate for the style of your audition. A modern spiky style is not appropriate for a Rodgers and Hammerstein musical, for example.

- Keep your hair off your face. Given that your face is a major tool of communication, you do not want to cover it. Particularly your eyes. We need to see them, always.

- If you must give your hairstyle an appropriate sense of character, then fine. Bunches, slicked back, spiked, back-combed, whatever; just be suggestive with your decision rather than overly obvious. The adage of 'less is more' is best. But, as with like clothing, unleashing tied-back hair during your song can be used for dramatic effect if done at the right moment.

- If you have a hairstyle that is a little outrageous – perhaps in cut or colouring – and you can't do anything to hide it, I strongly advise you to tell the casting director in advance that you are willing to dye it or have it cut as the role requires. It may be that the production cannot afford wigs and so you want to be sure that your look is not going to get you crossed off our lists. Make sure the team know in advance and we'll be able to see past your look and get to your talent.

- Wig pieces and extensions are fine, but if you wear a full wig, please make sure it's a good one. A bad hairpiece which decides to do its own choreography during your song has been known to have the entire panel crying with laughter into their notes.

- False moustaches, like wigs, may sometimes be appropriate if they are of good quality. I wore one on several occasions, partly to make myself look a little older, and I thought it rather suited the character. But think carefully about whether you should or shouldn't, and if in doubt, don't.

- False beards, however, can be disastrous. I've had several chaps (no women though, thankfully) choke during a song when a stray piece of their badly gummed beard got sucked in during a rather large intake of breath. Real beards are not necessarily required for roles, unless you have the time to grow one.

- Stubble and sideburns are fine so long as they're well groomed. I have asked some men (again, not women, thankfully) if they wouldn't mind shaving for the call-back, just to help them look younger or 'fresher'.

Make-up

Again – less is more. Be sensitive to the role you are going up for. For girls, a light day make-up is perfectly acceptable for most auditions. But please don't slap it on thick or try to make a statement, particularly for a period piece. Of course, if you *are* asked for something specific, then do your best to present yourself in the way you've been asked to. If you are auditioning on stage, then you can apply *slightly* more heavily.

Boys should not wear make-up at auditions unless a) you've been asked to or b) in rare circumstances on a massive, well-lit stage you may wish to help by applying a little light make-up on your skin and eyeline. Be subtle; it absolutely shouldn't be noticeable. But really, for men, the occasions are very rare and I suggest you don't bother.

Audition diary

There's one actor I've auditioned maybe six or seven times. I see him occasionally at various functions and he always introduces himself as if it's the first time we've ever met and never shows any sign of remembering who I am. While I wouldn't presume that I'm of any importance so that I *should* be remembered, the point is that not recognising or remembering someone who potentially could land you work is just daft. I was this chap at the beginning of *my* acting career, so I created an audition diary. Not a calendar diary as such, but a vital record of all my auditions and meetings. Over time, I could reference who I'd met and where, what I sang, what I wore, and when I got a call-back, etc., all of which was of great importance next time I got an appointment. It was an invaluable tool and one I urge you to try for yourself.

My sections in the diary were:

- the audition sections (as detailed below), which had page numbers – this was the bulk of the diary

- an A–Z creative team list – which was an alphabetical list of directors, casting directors, choreographers, musical directors, etc. who I'd met at auditions and events, and where I'd met them. As I auditioned for them I added the page number of that audition sheet next to their A–Z entry for easy future reference

- a notes section, for notes, feedback, songs I heard and liked

Create a table which allows you to write in key information.

1. A section for the **production**:

> Production:
> Role:
> Venue/Tour:
> Production Dates:
>
> and subheadings such as:
>
> Rehearsal dates:
> Performance dates:
> Finish date:
> Audition type: [ ] Singing [ ] Dancing [ ] Acting
> Recall audition date:
> Audition venue

2. A section for the **production team**:

[ ] Director ....

[ ] Musical Director ....

[ ] Choreographer ....

[ ] Casting Director ....

3. A section to record your **audition** including any notes you got from the creative team:

> What did I sing?
> What did I wear?
> How did it go?
> Feedback:

4. Finally, there should be a section where you record the **outcome** of the audition:

[ ] Call-back   [ ] Rejection   [ ] Unknown

The Audition Listing Page

AUDITION LISTING INDEX				
Date	**Production**	**Role**	**Pg**	**Outcome?**
				etc. ...

There should be about twenty pages of this template and each audition you do is noted here, with a page reference to the specific audition.

The Contact Template

B				
Name	Profession	Met where?	Date?	Audition pg
				etc. ...

There should be two sheets for each letter of the alphabet, and as you meet a director or casting director, they go in here.

The audition diary speaks for itself and you can make it as simple or as complicated as you like. But over time it will document your mistakes and triumphs and you'll see patterns of what works and what doesn't. And you'll never be in the position of forgetting someone when you meet them. How lovely to hear *'Oh hi, Neil. We met at the* Wicked *party. How's* South Pacific *going... ?'* And always take it with you so you can write the information in straight after your audition.

OK, time to go and audition.

Audition checklist basics

[ ] The address and telephone number of the audition venue

[ ] Your music folder with all the appropriate music in it

[ ] Any script or music that you've been sent

[ ] Several clean copies of your CV and picture, and business cards

[ ] A bottle of water

[ ] Any dance shoes and dance wear you may need

[ ] A towel and any toiletries you require for after your dance audition, including some spare underwear

[ ] Your wallet/purse and travel passes

[ ] Your audition diary

[ ] A pen and pencil

[ ] A brush and comb and any styling products you use

[ ] Some make-up for touching up

Oh, and

[ ] Your incredible talent (surprisingly, this is the one thing some actors completely forget to bring with them), together with a packet of confidence, an ounce of good

luck and a tonne of excitement. Oh, and a pinch of nervousness (that's what the spare undies were for ...).

LET'S AUDITION!

WORDS OF WISDOM

Clothing

Christopher Luscombe

Don't dress for the part. Some directors may disagree, but I find it a little alarming when actors turn up in full costume (and, worse, make-up!). I want to get to know you, and then see you transform into the character. Besides, it can smack of desperation, and we wouldn't want that. I've heard it said that it's good to wear the same outfit at each recall, as it helps fix your image in the director's mind. I think there's some sense in this. After a long day it can be hard to remember who's who, and anything which helps with that is good.

David Gilmore

Dress as if you have taken a bit of trouble. Boys especially; looking as if you stepped into clothes that were lying on the floor where you dropped them the night before is a poor start.

Stephen Mear

For dance, bring all dance wear, especially girls, tap shoes, jazz shoes, New Yorkers, etc.; better to have them than not. You don't always need to wear tracksuit bottoms. If it's a big dance show like *Crazy for You*, it's good for the girls to show their legs. Don't always wear black unless it's for something like Fosse; put something on that may catch the eye so you can be recognised even if it's a small coloured neckscarf to give that individuality, something to remember you by (nothing too over-the-top though!).

4

THE AUDITION

The phone goes …

'Darling? It's —'

'Hi Dorothy, yes. I'm on my way. Nice and early, feeling great, looking terrific. Really excited. Had a great session with that vocal woman you talked about. It's all good. I'll call you when I'm out.'

'You do that, darling. Have fun!'

———

Actors always ask me what's the most valuable piece of audition advice. Well, you know the answer by now: *preparation*. After that, I think that from the minute you walk into the room, you must 'own' (take control of) your audition. Whatever may happen in the audition room, you mustn't be thrown by it. Aside from presenting your material to the best of your ability (which of course is essentially the most important thing), you may be asked questions, or given direction by the panel. You need to be attentive, and once you've understood what it is the panel want, take control of your performance by making intelligent instinctive choices and performance-led decisions. It's about being confident in the work you've prepared before your audition, trusting your natural talent and performance instincts and then having the confidence to play with the team and have fun in their exploration of your talent. If you are asked to change something you've done, be brave:

try something new, work with your instincts, go a step further. Don't worry about going too far if they give you an exercise. It's much easier for a director to tone down a performance than it is to make you energise a performance. That's your responsibility.

Nerves

So there you are, on the way to your audition, with your songs going round and round in your head. Then suddenly, you can't remember a lyric. You go back a few lines and again, at the same place, the lyric goes completely. You've dried. You begin to sweat, your hands tremble, you feel your heart beginning to race as the panic sets in.

It's the first attack of the nerves.

I think that everyone you ask will tell you that they suffer from nerves to a greater or lesser degree, and over the next hour or so of your audition, you will almost certainly experience some kind of nervousness. Everyone has different ways to combat nerves, but let's be clear. The correct nerves are good. If you didn't have some nerves, it would suggest that you didn't really care about what you're doing. And you *should* care about your audition. Getting this job will stop you having to pull pints, tear tickets, bake pizzas or whatever else you have chosen to do to earn money, right? It matters, and it matters a lot. That's why you're nervous. You know that at least fifty other people are up for the same role as you, and three of them you know; they're terrific. Your rent is due. Christmas is round the corner. You want a holiday. And the car just failed its yearly check-up. And worst of all, you're having real trouble justifying to your parents that they were wise to pay your drama college fees when they really wanted you to 'get a proper job' and as yet they haven't seen you on stage once. If for no other reason, you need this job to justify that you are an actor. All these realities of life could be solved by getting this one job. It's a big deal.

But why are you nervous? Here are the most common reasons I hear.

- *I don't know my material well enough. I didn't prepare.*

- *I'll get everything wrong and so will the pianist.*

- *The casting director, director, etc. hate me.*

- *The pianist won't be able to play the song.*

- *I desperately need this job; the pressure's too much.*

- *The team will talk to me and I won't know what to say.*

Much of this chapter relates to the preparation you have already done and the control of nerves, as with your entire audition, relates directly to that. That's why preparation is so important. So let's look at how the points we've already discussed so far may answer these reasons for nerves.

- If you've worked hard on your material you really don't need to worry about getting it wrong. You'll be confident about how you're going to sing it; the chances of something going wrong are minimal. Your subconscious memory will kick in and support you.

- If you've warmed up properly, you don't need to worry about your voice. It will look after you if treated properly.

- If your music is prepared, you don't need to worry about the pianist; they'll know what to do and what to play.

- If you've done your background homework on the creative team, the production and your role, you can speak eloquently, knowledgeably and accurately about anything they ask you.

Let me tell you three other, vitally important points:

> **Every single member of the audition panel wants you to shine so that they can give you the job.**
> **The panel want you to be fantastic.**
> **The panel are all on your side.**

Trust me, we really don't want to sit through sixty auditions in a day and not be able to find anyone to cast. Instead, we want a page full of people to call back. We want you to be absolutely terrific and show us your abundant talent so that we can go away from the day assured that you're the best person to land the role. Yes, I know some casting panels look like death warmed up, and yes, I know some members of the panel can be rude, obstinate, uncommunicative and unapproachable. Nonetheless, we are certainly not 'out to get you'.

As a casting director I want you to shine more than anyone else. I chose you from thousands of submitted actors because I believe you are talented and because I believe you have something to offer us. It would reflect badly on me if I presented the creative team with people who are rubbish, wouldn't it? The fact that you're even in the room means that I think you're special.

Remember too that the outward physical symptoms of nerves are only a result of something psychological – get in the right place mentally and your outward physical nervous signs (dry throat, knocking knees, knots in your stomach, nausea, etc.) will become less prevalent. You are in control, but, if you can't stop those nerves, then use them. Use the intensity to add a greater emotion to your performance, or use that feeling to help launch you into that first wonderful phrase of your song.

OK, I'm prepared, I'm looking great and I believe you want me to do well. So why do I still have butterflies in my stomach?
Well, this may not be about nerves. It may be excitement. And that's great. This will give you energy and vibrancy. I suspect you just need to calm down a bit and focus.

- Close your eyes.

- Try to drown out any extraneous noise by listening to your breathing.

- Take five to ten slow, deep breaths.

- As you do, start to smile (yes, I know people around you will think you're a nutcase, but since your eyes are closed, you can't see them anyway). Smiling instantly makes you feel good.

- Also visualise again, standing in the middle of the room, singing your heart out, opposite a table full of smiling, attentive faces. As you finish your song, the whole table rise to their feet wildly applauding your outstanding performance. You give yourself a mental pat on the back as you thank the pianist and leave the room positively and assuredly.

The first-round singing audition

For the next few pages, we're going to go through a typical first-round singing audition, and along the way answer questions about common problems. Of course, much of this information also relates to further call-backs in the process, but we are specifically talking about the first singing audition here.

Arriving at the audition venue

When you arrive at the audition venue, you'll be directed to the audition waiting area where it's likely that either you'll be met by an audition monitor, who will take your name, or there'll be a sign asking you to take a seat and wait.

Remember Clipboard Boy from our original disaster story? The moral is, *be nice to everyone.* You have no idea if the audition monitor has a say in the final decision process. I have often specifically asked monitors to report back on anyone who was obnoxious, rude or disingenuous to their fellow actors while waiting for an audition.

I remember a specific audition where a well-known actor came in to audition for me. I happened to have stepped out of the audition room to make a phonecall, so that when he arrived, I was waiting outside the audition room so as not to disturb the audition taking place inside. I turned to greet him.

'Hi,' I said, 'we're running a little late, please take a seat.'

'Well, they'd better make up some time,' he replied rudely, assuming I was an assistant. 'I have another appointment in half an hour.'

'You are a little late. The person in there now was early so they took him first.'

'Well, whoever *you* are, I specifically called Neil Rutherford to tell him I was going to be late. He's a good friend, you know, and he said they'd wait for me.'

'Sorry. I'll tell Neil you're here.'

'Yep. He knows too I don't really want to do a musical. I'm a proper, leading actor, you know. Musicals just aren't my thing.'

'Really? Well, we'll see what we can do to make everyone feel better.' And so I did. I didn't tell him who I was and we rushed my 'good friend' (to whom I'd never spoken in my life) through his audition, but not before I made him sing the song in increasingly higher keys to 'test his range', and asked him to work on increasingly complicated vocal exercises. We really put him through his paces, and he was exhausted when he finished. Just knackered enough for his next meeting ... Be gone!

Waiting to audition

While you're waiting to go into the audition room, the first thing you should do is find out whether the team are behind schedule or not.

Be aware that auditions often overrun and you may have to hang around. This doesn't mean that you should be late for your appointment time, and indeed you should still aim to be there early. Why? Because we may have changed our brief and we may need time to give you new material.

But if auditions are running late, try to keep your focus and don't get involved in chitchat with other auditionees. Concentrate on your audition, and if those around you prevent you from doing so, then remove yourself to a quieter area in order to maintain your focus.

If you have another audition to attend and risk being late for it due to the late running of this audition, first politely ask the audition monitor and your fellow auditionees if you may jump the queue. Most people will say yes. If you can't change, however, then call your agent to inform the next audition you are going to be late or ask whether there is a possibility of rescheduling.

Regardless of whether auditions are running late or on time, it's your duty to *use this waiting time wisely*. So, while waiting to be called into the room:

- See how long it's anticipated to be before your audition.

- If there is time, then use this time to warm up and get focused.

- Ask if there is a warm-up room. If there is, tell the monitor that you'd like to go and warm up. They will normally ask you to be back in five minutes. Make sure they know where to find you.

- Be sure that while in your warm-up room, you can't be heard by those in the audition room. There's nothing worse for a panel than hearing a voice in the room next door when they are trying to listen to the one in front of them. And it's even worse if the person outside keeps murdering the same phrase and goes over it time and time again (only to still get it wrong in their audition).

- If you go and warm up, keep popping back so as not to miss your audition, and certainly be back in the waiting area just before the time of your appointment.

- Go to the bathroom, and check you look fantastic.

- I don't personally advise you to look at your music. Be confident in the preparation you've already done, and trust that when you're in front of the panel, all your hard work will fall into place.

- If you've not prepared, slap your wrist and look at your material.

- If you feel nervous, just close your eyes, breathe deeply and smile.

If you only have time to sit and wait, it's highly likely that other auditionees will be there waiting with you.

- *Be polite, but try not to engage in excessive banter.* Nerves do funny things to people, and some may not be able to stop talking. But I say again, you should use this time just before you go into the room to concentrate, focus and get into a mental state where you are confident and energised. It's not a time to gossip about colleagues and productions, catch up, etc. It's your time to focus.

I can hear the person who's currently in the audition room.

Try not to focus on that performance, or on the fact that you've already heard three songs, or on whether the performance is good or bad, or the fact that it's *your* song being sung so brilliantly. You've made your decision and you've worked hard on your material. Have faith that you also do it very well, so be confident in your choice and stick with it. A panicked change of song choice at this point is a serious mistake. So try to put everything in the background and continue to focus on your own positive thoughts. If you must listen, then listen to the important factors that may have relevance to your audition. Is the pianist good? Do the panel seem to be chatting with people? Is there an ambience to the room that may mean that you have to compensate a bit – is there heavy reverberation in the sound quality of the room or is it dead and dry?

Cripes! Someone's just walked out of the audition, ashen, in floods of tears and sobbing, 'That was awful; they're horrible.'

It's just their opinion – it doesn't mean anything other than it's not gone well for them. Take a deep breath, gather up your thoughts, your music, your confidence and your pride, and wait for your name to be called.

Entering the room

As your name gets called, take a deep breath and off you go. Remember your music!

All those extra belongings

You'll probably have other bags, a coat, maybe a suitcase, with you, particularly if you have other auditions or you're auditioning from being on tour. If you can, and it's secure to do so, leave any extra items outside the audition room. It's cumbersome having to take all your belongings into the audition room, and removing your coat and any other layers once you're in there takes up time and makes a poor first impression. So do all the necessary disrobing before you get into the room, so that it's just you, your music and a bottle of water that go in.

If you must take everything thing with you, then leave your belongings just inside the room by the door (or the proscenium if you're on a stage) prior to taking your starting position.

You might be announced by the audition monitor. Wait and then make your entrance.

If you're auditioning on a stage: walk confidently straight to the centre of the stage about five metres from the front. You may be able to detect a 'hot spot' of light – aim for the central lower half of that but be sure that there's light on your face. There's no point in giving a stunning audition if no one can see you.

It's almost certain that you won't be able to see the panel if the stage lights are up and they're in the auditorium. But you should be able to see the desk lights on the panel's table. Once you're there, smile and say, 'Good morning/afternoon/

evening. I'm ——' clearly and confidently (you'd be amazed how many people can't say their name properly!) and wait in case someone wants to talk to you first.

If you're auditioning in a studio or rehearsal space: walk confidently straight to the centre of the studio, about five metres from the panel. Smile and say, 'Good morning/afternoon/ evening. I'm ——' clearly and confidently, then wait in case someone wants to talk to you first.

This first impression is very important: the way you look, the way you sound and the way you behave. Have confidence, take control, remain focused and be attentive to the auditioning panel the whole time you're in the room.

Should I come into the room in character?

No, don't assume a character yet; be yourself. Being yourself is a very important factor, as it enables us to see a bit of you and how endearing you can be. Beware excitement; it can sometimes change your character, making you a little snappy, or perhaps too chatty. Watch out for being over-enthusiastic; someone who is over-excited, over-energised and spinning out of control can be a little too much for a team who are seeing their fortieth person in the day. Even so, there is something to be said for being bright and attentive – *particularly* if you're the fortieth person. So strike the balance and you should be fine.

Should I shake the panel's hands and greet each one individually?

Unless you are prompted to do so, then no; a pleasant greeting (with beaming smile and a nod of the head) to the entire table is all that's required. If you audition for me, I will normally greet you at the door, and introduce you to whoever is on the panel. Some other casting directors may not do this, in which case, having greeted the panel, just hold your ground and wait a few moments.

They look an evil bunch. Do all panel members have horns and a tail?

Yes, some do. But please understand that for most panel members, we're concentrating to see where you might possibly fit in our production. If there are no welcoming acknowledgements, then don't worry. You're going to wow them with your talent soon, so don't let any stern looks put you off. We take our jobs seriously, and it isn't always a barrel of laughs, particularly in a long day when we've overrun, not had a decent lunch and are all bursting for the toilet. Just ride through it and we'll soon cheer up if you're what we're looking for.

I know one or more of the panel personally. Should I acknowledge them?

First, sense the mood of the room and then let an acquaintance make the first move of familiarity. If they stand to give you a hug, then reciprocate. But keep any personal chitchat to an absolute minimum. It might be that they don't acknowledge you. That doesn't mean that your friendship is over and you're off the Christmas card list, but just that they need to observe a sense of impartiality; in a post-audition discussion when we begin to discuss each individual audition, it can be problematic when trying to fight for someone when everyone knows you have a personal acquaintance. Of course, during such discussions everyone aims to act professionally, but sometimes having a personal acquaintance with an auditionee can change the outcome, for good or bad. So if you're ignored, don't worry. It probably doesn't mean anything other than that your friend is being ultra-professional. I've had several close actor friends call me after an audition session asking if they've done something to upset me. Far from it; I've just needed to judge the situation and the mood of the audition panel and act without apparent bias.

You may now be asked to talk about yourself, either by the director or the casting director.

- Be as natural as you can be – this is as much part of your audition as your songs, dancing and scene work. Remain focused and engaged throughout. You are probably being asked the questions because we want to get a sense of you as an individual: what you have to say as an individual, how approachable you are, how interesting you are, how knowledgeable you are.

- Listen to the questions you are being asked and answer them appropriately and concisely. No waffling and no hesitations. Answer every question with a polite manner. A smile and pleasant demeanour, and certainly a laugh, go a long, long way.

- If you get asked *'What have you been up to recently?'*, and you haven't worked for a while, don't say, *'Nothing much!'*. Be positive, be creative. So say that your last theatre job was such and such, but you've been taking some time out to write a novel, or some songs, or poetry, or teaching, or planning a concert, or working on your new album, or whatever else you have done that shows energy, commitment, aspiration and positivity.

- Don't lie. Don't claim to have done something if you didn't, or worked with a director who has been dead for sixty years when you're only thirty ... (yes, I have had that happen – I've also had actors claim to be in shows *I was in* when they weren't).

- Make sure that you engage everyone on the panel. But

don't be too chummy – it can be awfully irritating.

- Be interested in what is being said. Don't fake it – genuinely listen and learn.

- Keep your answers brief. If you talk too much you risk not getting the opportunity to sing that second song because time will have run out. You should aim to show off your talent as soon as you can.

- If you get asked about the production and the role, be positive. If you've prepared your background to the piece then you'll appear to be truly interested in the project and have done your homework; the team will be impressed by that.

- But don't appear over-confident. There's a fine line between confidence and arrogance. Acknowledge that the director has the right to disagree with your interpretation, but that you have at least thought about the role. Be respectful.

- Don't complain about other performers, managements, producers, directors or companies – bitching is not allowed at any point and I have had several auditionees get a cross on their sheet even before they've sung a note simply because they have just spoken badly about the director's best friend.

- Avoid unnecessary flattery of the team, and if you're praised, accept it graciously with thanks.

- Don't remind anyone on the panel that they have previously rejected you for a role.

Should I ask the director or casting director questions?
Only ask questions if you don't understand what is being asked of you. Other than that, for this first round, don't ask anything

else. Wait until the call-back, where asking questions is to be encouraged.

Time to sing!

At the end of the chat, you will probably be asked what you've brought to sing.

> **Only offer your best song first. You will have prepared another and you have your whole portfolio with you, but if you offer the panel a choice they may pick the one you least want to do. So don't risk it.**
> **Offer them the one that is going to land you the call-back.**

'I'd like to sing ——' and then start to make your way to the piano. If you've been smart with your choice, the likelihood is that we won't contradict you and will let you get on with it. If we don't want you to sing that song, then we'll ask for something else. Don't be flustered. Offer your next appropriate song. If you're prepared, your other choices will be equally familiar and as good as your first.

I've stood there for a minute. No one has acknowledged me. Should I cough?

We work at breakneck speed in first rounds and there is never enough time to write down all the notes. So apologies if everyone's head is down a lot or we're finishing off conversations about the person before you. If, after a short while, no one has acknowledged you, then you should announce yourself confidently and strongly. *'Hello, I'm Neil Rutherford.*

And I'd like to sing "Any One Can Whistle" ...' hold a second, in case someone speaks, and if not, then walk over to the piano and give the pianist your music. By the time you get back to the centre spot everyone should have finished their notes and previous chitchat ready for you to start.

Your time with the pianist

Assuming you are using the pianist employed by the production company, then you can spend a little bit of time (fifteen seconds or so) with your friend the pianist. Find out their name in advance, introduce yourself and be polite. They are there to help you make a success of this audition. Of course, if you've prepared your music properly, then you just need to point out the key musical moments that require specific attention:

- repeats

- cuts

- pauses

- breaks

- and, most importantly, starting tempo (speed) and any changes throughout the music. Remember that your heart will probably be racing a bit and you may unintentionally suggest a slightly quicker tempo than you really meant to. The best way to correct this is for you to sing a little bit to the pianist – your opening few bars and then a few bars of any tempo changes.

Now is not the time to double-check that the pianist's music is in the right order. You should have done that before.

Should I take my own pianist?

Only once did I ever take my own pianist for a very important audition where I wanted to do a particularly fiendish song which I thought was perfect for the character. I hired a pianist I knew, and we worked on the song in advance. We then went to the audition and indeed it went very well. Afterwards, the casting director said that the panel were slightly offended that I had brought my own pianist, which – to them – suggested that I didn't think that they were capable of hiring good people. Well, of course that wasn't my intention, but I can understand why they were a little miffed.

For nearly all the major casting directors and companies, you will have good pianists. I have three or four who I use regularly and they can play anything (anything that you've marked up correctly and communicated properly, that is). For other auditions, there may be less certainty of having a brilliant accompanist and so your choices of song may be slightly restricted.

I would therefore advise that in general you should not take your own pianist – some people won't mind, others will. As a safeguard, write down the pianist's name after your audition (preferably in your audition diary) and then when you next get a call to audition ask your agent to find out who the pianist is, and if you've had them play for you before you can make a decision as to what to do.

What about CD accompaniment on a CD player or unaccompanied songs? Or self-accompaniment?

It's not generally acceptable for you to use pre-recorded accompaniment for a professional musical theatre audition as a substitute for the pianist. Neither should you sing unaccompanied. We need to know you can sing in tune, and in the same rhythmic tempo as the live accompaniment. Self-accompaniment on a guitar or piano is not to be encouraged, although if it's a last resort to show us a different aspect of your voice for which you don't have piano music, then OK. Auditioning for actor/musician productions is of course different. You will be expected to play your prime instruments at such auditions, and may be asked to accompany yourself, or someone else, at some point in the process.

Once you and your pianist are happy, let the pianist know what you're going to do right at the beginning of the song, and when to start the introduction. This can be a simple nod, or a more definite 'choreographed' moment. But make it clear. If you don't do this, the default for an accompanist will be to start when you reach the centre of the room again.

Should I re-announce my name and song?

There are some traditionalists who believe that before you sing, you need to reintroduce your name, song and the musical it's from. If you've already said what song you want to sing, and we already know your name since it's on our sheets, then just announce the title again. If you have changed the context to fit the show or character (as we have discussed in the previous chapter) now's the time to explain briefly, in one sentence, what your new context is. Give your pianist the nod and off you go.

Is there one type of song that it's better to present first in order to grab the panel's attention?

The short answer is present a song that shows you off at your best and is fitting for the character for which you're auditioning. A song which shows you can sing, shows you can act, shows a wide range of ability, shows that you are energised, committed, smart – everything in fact that we've talked about so far in this book. You have one brief opportunity to show how brilliant you are and the first impressions you create must be good ones.

It's arguably better to start with a bright number – an upbeat narrative and good positive sense of personality – than a passionate but heart-rending ballad. Of course, this is entirely dependent upon the character you are auditioning for as well as your own individual vocal talents. But given a choice, go with something up-tempo first.

Acting through song

Acting through song, not just singing, is paramount in musical theatre. This means that throughout the song, right from the first note, you must be in character, displaying a sense of emotion, setting and situation within a narrative context.

Always, always, always remember that when auditioning for a musical theatre project you are required to portray a character within a dramatic situation and as such you must always act within your songs. In your preparation, you should have answered key character questions which set the dramatic tone, emotional context and setting of your songs and your characters.

By continually asking questions and making choices relating to the character's dramatic situation, you will be acting through the song, rather than just singing it. Some songs require a lot of questioning and almost every word can have several meanings; others are fairly straightforward. Go back to Chapter 2 to remind yourself how this can be achieved.

Remember too that the acting doesn't stop when you have nothing to sing, such as during the opening and closing bars and instrumental sections. The drama continues throughout the song.

Using your introduction and endings

So many actors forget about the accompaniment introduction of their song. First, it shouldn't be too long – two to four bars is sufficient. Second, you must not fidget, cough, stretch, or look at the floor or the pianist. You must act through the introduction. The introduction is vitally important in conveying your character's situation and setting the mood and scene. You might use it to place the focus of a character you are going to sing to. Perhaps you might suggest the movement of the character to whom you're going to sing by watching that (imaginary) character move, perhaps even go towards them a little, just to cement in our minds where they are, and that you're going to be singing to someone. Or perhaps you can evoke a setting within which you are placing your character; if it's winter in your song, use the introduction to pull your jumper around you a little tighter. Use the lyrics of your song to help you act through your introduction. Doing nothing is uninspiring. Being smart and using your introduction sets the scene, gives focus and makes sense of what you are about to sing.

Endings too are important; either hold the 'moment' at the end of the song until the last chords on the piano have died away, or, if you're not singing right up to the end, is there some physical ending that you can close your song with? Sitting on a chair? Making a move towards your imaginary character? It must be subtle, not naff, and it must be right for the piece, but don't forget those introductions and endings; they're very important in telling us that you're a performer in control.

Speaking during your song

It's perfectly OK to speak in character during the introduction, or indeed at other points in your song. If you've found a line or two of appropriate dialogue which cleverly provides a context for us, great. Some well-chosen words from the show's libretto can be very helpful, but only a few sentences. And of course remember to mark clearly in your music the full dialogue and the point at which the pianist needs to start playing.

The pianist has started too fast. What should I do?

First of all, if a professional accompanist is doing something wrong, it probably means that your communication wasn't clear enough. If, however, your pianist has started either too fast or too slow, keep singing firmly and confidently at the tempo you want, and remain within character and within your performance. Normally a good pianist will quickly match your tempo over the next few bars. If the pianist stays at the wrong tempo, then simply stop singing, turn to the pianist and politely ask to adjust the tempo to the correct one.

Which leads me on to a new rule:

No matter what happens or who is at fault, always remain calm and pleasant. Don't fuss, don't blame, just move on.

Things do go wrong occasionally, but never let your professional guard down. Take full responsibility for your audition and it will show you're a pro. I've had any number of auditions where a pianist has dropped music, played wrong chords, mis-turned a page, and sometime had to stop completely. Assuming it's no fault of yours (i.e. you've prepared everything to the very best of your ability) you must simply carry on, regardless of any other commotion that may be going on to the side of you (except fire alarms, of course – several times a singer has just carried on, determined to get to the end before being rescued!). If there's a problem at the piano, you must absolutely not glare at the pianist with murderous eyes, make threats, tut, roll your eyes to the ceiling and make other exclamations indicating how appalling the pianist's performance is. And if the pianist is truly bad, the panel will know it and make allowances.

Never apologise

This may seem an odd piece of advice, but whatever goes wrong in your audition, never apologise. If you forget lines, just deal with it by going back and starting again. If your voice lets you down and you croak, splutter, dry up, etc., don't apologise. If you're ill, if you're under-prepared, if you're simply not on form, don't apologise. If you didn't have time to learn the material, if someone stole all your music, if your new-born baby kept you up half the night, don't apologise. We'll know you've mucked up if it's really obvious and an apology will only make it worse because you are acknowledging how under-prepared, careless and unprofessional you are. And if there's a genuine reason for you giving a potentially poor audition, then speak to your agent first and ask them to let us know. Within the audition room it's much better to remain confident and assured. And remember that there's a good chance we missed your mistake completely, so to draw attention to a mistake when we didn't realise you'd made one isn't too smart. That said, if the director asks you how you thought you did, and you know you messed up, apologise and ask if you can repeat the bit where you made the error. The exception to the rule is if you're rude – rudeness does need to be apologised for, always.

The first thirty seconds

Have you ever watched a TV reality show such as *The X Factor*, *Pop Idol* or similar, and made a quick judgement about whether you think the person will get through to the next round? Well, in essence it's a similar experience to what the panel goes through. First impressions count and those first thirty seconds of your performance have to be captivating. The phrase 'Save the best till last' cannot apply to auditions. That's not to say you shouldn't also have a fabulous finish, but you must engage with us fully in those opening bars so that we make a positive assessment of you from the outset. When planning your song, think about those initial moments and what you can do to be unique. I'm not talking about extremes – I've had people strip, I've had people sit on panel members' laps, I've had people give us sweets and flowers during their song – no, that's just desperation and has little to do with talent. I'm talking about intelligent performance-based decisions, which can instantly draw us in and make us think, *'OK, here's someone who is a little bit different, classy, exceptional.'*

The ways in which you can achieve this are numerous; I offer some examples of recent good auditions to help you think about how your opening thirty seconds might set you apart from others.

* *Using the room.* Do you need to start at the centre of the room? If you're singing a torch song, could you start at the piano, comfortably leaning against it? Or if it's a sad ballad, perhaps you might start crouched in the corner of a room. Is there a mirrored wall in the room you could use to help set a context? You must – of course – be sure that the whole panel can see you, that you are in light, and that your pianist knows that you are not going to start in the centre of the room. Neither should you stay

in that position too long. And certainly finish centre as it's a 'strong' position for you to complete your song. But in using the extremities of the room you are being unique – not many use the space they are in, preferring to be solidly rooted as if there is an imaginary 'X' on the floor. Of course, on a stage this may be impractical and you will have to ascertain the best performance area as determined by the lighting.

- *Can you remove part of the accompaniment?* I recently gave a masterclass with an actor who sang Queen's 'Somebody to Love'. She was an amazingly brave performer and in the context she had chosen for her presentation the middle sections of her song were hugely energised, frustrated and passionate. In order to show a range of her talents, I suggested she might open the song a cappella (without accompaniment), taking her time over the opening lyrics, singing right from her heart, and keeping very honest and real. We then brought the piano accompaniment in subtly before the first verse started. It was simple yet completely captivating, and rather than just showing one aspect of her talents (a little crazy and comic), it focused her performance down to a deep intensity which then allowed her to go a little broader before finishing off the song in a similar way to how she had opened it. I wouldn't advise you to take this kind of step with material from the show at a call-back, but in a first singing round you can certainly be inventive with your material in order to break out from the norm. Be sure you have marked your music appropriately if you intend to make such changes.

- *Change the tempo of a song.* It can often be really interesting to drastically change the tempo of a well-known song, if not all the way through, just to open your song, particularly taking an up-tempo number and giving it a ballad or blues feel. Again, be sure to make the necessary changes to your music for the pianist. Such a change may also mean that you require a completely new arrangement, but sometimes it's worth it.

- *Use dialogue*. We have already touched upon this earlier, but allowing a few cleverly selected sentences of speech, in character, can do wonders to set up your context.

- And again, as previously discussed, *give your song a new context*. I recently had an actor sing Avenue Q's 'If You were Gay' as if advice from a father to a son. It was really clever, very funny, and worked a treat in terms of his fitting a song within the world of the musical for which he was auditioning.

These are a few of many ideas which, if confidently and sensitively employed, may set you apart from others. Remember that the panel may have already heard your song five times that day, not to mention the fact that it's incredibly exhausting watching song after song for nine hours a day with actors coming in at ten-minute intervals. If you can find a unique way to present your song which doesn't resort to gimmicks, then you'll have done yourself a great service. The panel may not necessarily like the direction in which you've decided to take the song, but they will admire you for taking an initiative not to sing it like everyone else, and make yourself remembered.

Do remember, though: above all it's your talent that will ensure you are remembered – and exciting talent is about taking your natural gifts and working hard to improve them, nurturing them and then using them to prepare your material in the most exciting, innovative, entertaining and captivating way. So long as your talent is given the opportunity to shine, you'll be a great credit to yourself.

And try not to present the panel with what you *think* they want to see. It's likely you won't be able to second-guess them, and by trying to do so, you won't be concentrating on the quality of your performance. Present what you think is most appropriate for the audition. 'Simple' is often best.

False starts and forgetting

There will be occasions throughout your auditioning career when you make a false start, or simply forget your words – known as 'drying'. In the first instance, try to carry on. While it may have been a complete disaster from your point of view, it's possible that the panel haven't noticed. Even if we have spotted your mistake, you'll be admired if you manage to keep going rather than collapsing in a heap on the floor in floods of tears. If your mistake is simply impossible to overcome, then just stop. Don't go into lots of excuses, but ask the pianist to start again at an appropriate place. The panel may wish you to start again from the beginning (often called 'the top' of the song) or pick up a couple of bars before you went wrong. But, most importantly, don't get in a state. It happens: people forget things and you have one opportunity to start over again. Only once though; if you forget your words several times, change the piece (and prepare better for next time!).

Eyeline

Where to look in an audition is a constant discussion point in all my masterclasses and workshop sessions, and different people have varying opinions. I know one senior UK casting director who cannot abide anyone singing to him. I personally rather like being sung to. The fact is there's no right or wrong, but I would suggest that there is a middle ground which is the most satisfactory. In an audition room, do a bit of everything – throughout your song, engage with the whole panel for a couple of bars each, then play to the room on the dramatic moments, then back to the panel and play the room again if it's a big finish.

Some points of note:

- Be aware that a panel may be uncomfortable with you looking at them; if so, take your focus somewhere else. Don't hold an individual's attention for more than a couple of bars at a time.

- When not looking at the panel and playing to the room, place your focus at least a metre above their heads. It's often disconcerting to have someone focus just above your hair-line when you're not entirely sure if they're actually looking at you or have problems with their eyes.

- Try not to get flummoxed when a member of the team breaks your loving gaze by writing their notes; similarly, if none of the team are looking at you, then play out to the room.

- When playing to the room, imagine that you are on stage and use the whole back wall. Don't just focus on one single spot as it looks as if you're possessed by the Devil.

Exceptions are:

- *Singing to another character.* If your song is sung to an imaginary character, you must maintain a focused eyeline that references that character. Don't always place the character dead centre of the room, nor at an angle where you will be in profile. If you imagine the panel as being at a position about twelve o'clock on a clock face lying horizontally, then either the ten o'clock or two o'clock position for your focus is about right, facing the panel. And, for a change, try to make that imaginary character move across the room at points in your song. During an emotional ballad, it can be perfect to have your character move at a particularly dramatic point; your gaze must follow them, of course, and occasionally a subtle move from you may add to the effect. As an exercise, have a look at some of the recitative moments of 'Tell Me on a Sunday' when the character is confronting a friend or partner. See how you can make that imaginary character move throughout the room and how you can maintain your focus.

- Try to avoid the rather obvious but unhelpful device of placing an empty chair centre of your audition space, with its back to the panel, and singing to it as if there were someone sitting in the chair. Not only is it less exciting than creatively placing your own character elsewhere in the room, but it tends to mean your head is lowered, and thereby your eyeline, preventing us from getting a good look at your face, and also potentially ruining your posture and possibly your vocal technique. If you look away from that character, you have to come back to the same place when you look at them again.

- *Accusatory songs.* If there is an accusatory tone or a negative tone to the song, don't make eye contact with the panel. Even if the song is sung to a group of people, for example some of the courtroom songs from Jason Robert Brown's *Parade*, then these should be sung out, and not at the panel. But still use your focus to suggest a group of people.

- *Love songs.* Unless you are out to specifically seduce a member of the panel (not a very smart idea) then avoid singing love songs to them, particularly to members of your own sex. Most panel members will be highly embarrassed. I, however, will probably stare you out ... and I generally win. Don't risk it, and play to an imaginary character instead. Remember too that your character may be embarrassed about expressing love and that in turn will alter the eyeline when playing to an imaginary character. Your character may not, for example, feel able to say certain things to the other character, and look away. Do, however, keep coming back to that character in order to physically place them in the room.

- *Comedy songs.* Generally, focus on the panel for humorous songs. But be warned – it's extremely difficult to play a comedy song in an audition since we are a difficult bunch to make laugh. It's not that we don't like a good laugh, but we are concentrating on lots of elements of your performance, and unlike an audience who are there to be entertained, the panel is there to ascertain your suitability for work. Most of us, however, will be positive during a comedy song, and encourage you by smiling. But if we don't, try not to get worried and over-compensate by becoming ridiculously funny or 'big' in your performance. Indeed, often the more subtle your comedy, the more you are likely to get a response from us. Anything overplayed is rather tiresome.

- *On a stage.* You are unlikely to be able to focus on individual members of the panel when auditioning on stage (unless they are on the stage with you). As a general rule, if auditioning on a stage with the panel in the auditorium, play out as if you were in performance. Again, don't ever focus on a single spot; move your focus around the space.

Performance levels

If you're auditioning on the stage of a large theatre you're obviously going to 'sell' your song in a different way. It needs to be slightly bigger, broader and louder. However, the performance level of how you deliver your song on a stage will seem over the top for a small studio and most likely the acoustic will not be conducive to you singing at the same volume. Dance studios particularly are often quite 'boomy' and reverberate your sound, making diction difficult to hear, particularly if you are singing a big-belt number. Indeed, I have occasionally been deafened for several minutes by a big voice in a small space with an overly ambient acoustic. In a studio, therefore, your vocal volume needs to creep down a few notches, but just because the volume needs monitoring, it doesn't mean you should lose your energy and commitment to the song. 'They have no energy' is one of the most common things I hear from the panel.

Choreography and movement within songs

In the first singing round, keep your choreography to an absolute minimum when singing. Even during a song which is traditionally (and within the context of the musical) a 'dance number', be restrained in showing off your choreographic and prancing prowess. The choreographer and panel will ascertain everything dance-based we require of you from a dance call, and if the production is particularly dance-heavy, then we'll probably be doing the dance call first and *then* seeing if you can sing. So save the routine for when you need it, and not during a singing audition.

Neither, though, should you stand there like a dummy. Find dramatic-led moments where a move is appropriate, or the lyric demands a move, and if your song requires and benefits from you being on different levels other than standing, it's perfectly OK for you to kneel or sit, so long as you don't remain in that position throughout the whole song. (And getting up from the floor can look cumbersome – you need to find a way to get up effortlessly.)

Watch those arms and legs too; when you're nervous, arms tend to have a life of their own, flapping like wings in up-tempo numbers and counting out the rhythm in ballads. Dancers often 'beat' each bar with the same hand gesture. Legs shake too, uncontrollably sometimes. I've never been able to provide a cure for these movements other than by trying to eliminate as many negative nervous elements to your performance as possible, but at least arms tend to be more controllable if you know what you're doing with them. Once you decide on specific, dramatic-led, appropriate, minimal arm gestures, then they tend not to surprise you by moving by themselves. Similarly, if you invest fully in the dramatic context of the song, you'll find that your body will be physically more in tune with your emotional dramatic needs rather than taking on a life of its own.

Furniture and props

It's sometimes appropriate to use a chair during your presentation, particularly for ballads that start off fairly quietly and grow. Or songs that are personal and lonely. Don't stay in the chair all the time; find the appropriate dramatic moment in your song where you can get up from the chair. And try not to have the chair positioned flat and straight on to the panel. Place it slightly at an angle. But be sure that everyone on the panel can see your face.

I would generally advise against props unless they are small and practical, and you really need to use them. So, it's OK to have a glass when singing 'Ladies Who Lunch' from Sondheim's *Company*, so long as you drink from it. And it's OK to use a mobile for phonecall songs. But I've had several auditions ruined by people dropping props, having too many props, breaking props, etc. So unless your prop is simple and absolutely necessary, leave it at home and mime. And if you really must use a prop, then rehearse with it so you are completely comfortable.

Being stopped during your song

In the UK, Europe and Australia you would normally be able to sing your first song in its entirety, although this may not always be the case depending on who you're auditioning for and where.

In America, it's still common in a first round with only the casting director and musical director present to hear the best sixteen or thirty-two bars of your song. Even at later stages of the process this may be the case, so you need to be fully prepared for both a short and long scenario. And choose those bars wisely, as discussed in Chapter 2.

Most audition panels will stop you during a song only if they've heard enough to make a judgement and are running late, or if you have messed up and they would prefer you to start again. If you are stopped, you mustn't take it personally and start to panic. Just wait for further instructions from the panel and act upon them calmly and confidently.

Your second songs

If you are asked to perform a second song, it's because we want to explore something else from you – a further investigation of your vocal talents, or how you handle something specific we're after with contrasting material. Before choosing which song you think might suit, ask what elements the team wish to explore, and then choose a song that best shows this off. You may also be asked to shorten this second song; if so, then as we discussed earlier, it's wise to have already prepared a shortened version which encompasses the best musical moment for you. This should be about a minute long (or the final page). Have this marked already in your music, but be sure to explain to the pianist what you need, and where to play from, highlighting cuts or jumps to the coda to finish your piece. If you're really conscientious, then I'd advise for all your major songs, that you also prepare minute-long versions, but in truth, if you've prepared, you can just take your full version and shorten it there and then.

Beware the prying eyes of the musical director

It's often the case that a musical director may wish to have a look at your entire music portfolio in order to ascertain a certain element of your voice through one of your other songs. You must be sure that everything within your folder you can do well, and so if there is a song in there which you are very rusty on, then take it out before the audition; if you don't it's certain to be the one the musical director picks! On those rare occasions where they do pick a song you've not sung for ages, then be honest: say you haven't sung it for a long time and ask to stand at the piano where you can see the lyrics. I also had lyrics sheets for each of my songs for such an occasion, so that I could at least hold something as a prompt if I needed it, away from the piano.

Scales

If your song hasn't already shown us your full range, we may ask you to sing some scales. Normally these will be simple scales, with piano accompaniment, getting higher or lower depending upon which notes you need to be able to reach. Many actors suddenly clam up when scales are asked for. So don't get flustered; sing your scales confidently, listen to the set tempo and try to go as high/low as you can. Remember to breathe well before each scale and take your time. Don't rush. If you crack a note, don't worry. Stop, recompose yourself and try again. It's a good idea to add these exercises to your own vocal workout at home so that next time in the audition room you can perform scales with familiarity and ease.

Sorry, but panels *will* talk during your audition

Chat during your songs can be extremely offputting, particularly if you're not expecting it. It's almost certain that at some point during your audition, some members of the panel will talk, write, read or flick pages. Just carry on regardless and pretend nothing has happened, ignoring all these little distractions; you can easily be put off and make mistakes. Please don't think that we're not concentrating; it's just that we need to discuss and write down notes so we don't forget you and ensure we're getting everything we need from you.

Make a song your own

Unless your audition is specifically to play a real-life character (such as Buddy Holly, Elvis, Frank Sinatra, Frankie Valli, etc. – all of whom appear in current biographical-style musicals) then avoid singing songs in the same way as the famous recording artists. While I'm happy to listen to the expert vocal talents of Barbra Streisand, Judy Garland, Josh Groban, Sting, Lulu, Tina Turner, to name but a few, it's much better in an audition room to give your own interpretation of a song as opposed to other artists' iconic recordings. For a start, if you do try to do a copy, we will inevitably begin to compare, which is dangerous. And second, your own interpretation is likely to be more appropriate for your voice. A particular example is Eva Cassidy's stunning version of Harold Arlen's classic 'Over the Rainbow'; her version has now become a standard for female auditions and only very few have sung it as well as Eva's recording. It's also melodically different from the original song. In almost all cases, it's better to take the original and make it your own.

Getting out of the room

Once you have finished your song, you may well be asked further questions, in which case answer them as concisely and professionally as you can, and then someone will indicate that the audition is over. *'Thank you, that's all we need for today.'*

Or you may be asked to come back later in the day, or you may be asked to join a dance audition later on. Do listen carefully to what's said at the end of the audition. Many times in a room I have given a call-back appointment for later in the day which was missed because the actor was on a high from having finished the audition, and they didn't listen to what I had said afterwards.

At the end of the audition, always thank the team for seeing you (don't shake everyone's hand) and thank the pianist (by name). Remembering to collect your music from the pianist, make a confident exit – preferably out of the correct door. I've had several actors do fantastic auditions only to open a door and walk straight into the broom cupboard.

Be remembered for the right reasons
Be remembered for your shining talent, not your eccentricity.

If you've done all your hard preparation work and you give a terrific audition, that's all you can do. Any call-backs or eventual contracts are in the hands of the panel and many specific factors (which we'll look at in the next chapter). But don't be remembered for gimmicks, rudeness, arrogance, poor presentation and other inappropriate behaviour. Let your talent shine through at your very best ability and you can leave the room in the knowledge that whatever the panel think, you have given your all.

The dance call

I must admit that dance was not my strong point when I was an actor. I have therefore included several large paragraphs from choreographers Stephen Mear, Joey McKneely, Christopher Gattelli and Bill Deamer at the end of this chapter purely on *Dance Auditions* to give you further tips and advice.

Having spent my life, however, with both musical theatre dancers and ballet dancers, and sat on the panel of numerous dance auditions, the advice here is therefore geared towards the audition experience rather than technique.

In advance of your dance call, and particularly if you are a first-class dancer, I reiterate that you must take regular classes in all disciplines to keep your skills intact, your body in prime condition and your mind sharp in order to learn and remember routines quickly. Your local dance centres, gyms, trade papers and magazines will be the best place to find out where dance classes are being held for professional dancers. The internet will also provide many more sites and opportunities. You should try to attend jazz, ballet, contemporary and tap classes regularly. If you also excel in certain areas of speciality dance then fine, but be sure to take a 'refresher' class if you haven't worked on a specific style for a while. Understanding as many styles of dance as possible is a major factor in gaining regular work, and in the same way as understanding styles of music and acting, it is your responsibility to discover and absorb as much as you can.

Preparation also extends to eating healthily, drinking lots of water as part of your diet, regular cardiovascular and weights exercise, and keeping yourself in prime condition. Indeed, you don't just have to be a dancer to aim for this kind of lifestyle but it's certainly important for those aiming to make dance a feature of their performance career. Many people find the Alexander Technique, the various forms of yoga, and Pilates techniques also a key part of their wellbeing regime.

The dance audition

Once you get your dance audition call time, you should aim to arrive at least fifteen or twenty minutes beforehand in order to give your body a thorough warm-up by stretching all the major muscle groups. This is incredibly important and unlike your pre-prepared songs, you may not know what the choreographer is going to put you through. It's your responsibility to ensure you are fully warmed up and ready to take on the routine you'll be taught. I personally would also advise using this time to focus and prepare mentally as well as physically.

Some casting directors use a number system whereby you'll be given a numbered sticker to wear. I don't care for this system very much at private dance calls – you're not a number in my eyes – although for open dance calls where the sheer number of dancers can reach many hundreds then a number system is useful.

Most dance auditions take the following format:

- There will be thirty or so dancers in each audition

– sometimes graded by skill, sometimes not. It could be a mixed group of talent, although nearly always the same sex, unless partnering work is a key feature of the production.

- There may initially be a requirement to do a simple dance step (such as a pirouette, turning to the left and the right) after which some people maybe asked to leave (known as 'the cut'). For those leaving that's likely to be the end of the road for now.

- Of those remaining, the entire group will be taught a dance routine, probably by the resident/assistant choreographer or dance captain. At this point you'll be in several lines, rotating those at the front to the back so that everyone can see clearly. If it's a long routine, it will be taught in segments and then stitched together. Rarely is there music at this point either; the tempo is normally slow so that you can pick up the steps. Questions can be asked and the teacher will begin to refine detail further.

- While learning the routine, it is tempting to 'mark' the routine, i.e. not give 100 per cent energy to the dance. Other than high kicks or big arm movements (which in a tight, large group may be dangerous), try not to hold back your energy as it can suggest laziness. It's also vital to make sure the feet know what they're doing, and this means doing the routine full out.

- Once the routine has been taught (normally about thirty to forty minutes, depending on the complexity) the group will then be split in half and you'll begin to work the routine with the music (piano and possibly drums), again normally under tempo. Gradually, the tempo of the music will reach its intended speed and each group will take it in turns to dance the routine. During these sessions further questions can be answered and once again further attention to specific detail is given.

- The next stage is the 'show', where you will be split into groups of three or four and present the routine to the panel, which at this point will normally consist of the choreographer and their assistants, the director, the casting director and maybe the musical director.

- In the small group, some will be upstage and some downstage and the group will normally dance the routine twice (swapping upstage people to downstage and vice versa) until everyone in the room has danced the routine.

- There may then be some deliberation and different combinations of people may be chosen to present the routine again.

- Dancers may also be required to show other skills, such as a timestep (tap), pointe work (ballet) or a short routine for eight to sixteen beats crossing the room, or from corner to corner on a diagonal.

- After everyone has presented the routine, there is normally what is called 'the cut', whereby certain dancers may be asked to leave and others to stay in order to dance a new routine focusing on a different skill, or work again on a longer version of the original routine. If you're asked to leave the room, it normally means that you haven't got through to the next stage. That doesn't always mean you are out of the running completely (we may be considering you for a non-dancing role, but just needed to see that you can at least move well), but it probably means that we don't need to see you dance any more for the time being.

Useful tips for dance auditions

- Never be late for a dance call – if you lose half an hour of learning the routine, you will be severely disadvantaged.

- Try to pick up as much of the style of dance as you can. If you can throw your leg high, that's great, but if the style doesn't demand it, it's irrelevant, and you may even be marked down for it. Having a real sense of where the parameters of stylistic movement are is much more important; work on the detail of the routine rather than showing off a move that is not required.

- In the final recap of the routine, just before you present it in your small group, be sure to dance full out as much as space allows. I've seen awful situations where dancers have 'marked' the routine for almost an hour, and then when they finally come to present the routine, their placement of weight is all wrong now that they are giving it 100 per cent. Marking is OK for high kicks and arms as you learn the routine, but you must have a few runs at 100 per cent full energy in order to make certain physical choices.

- Ask questions about the detail of the routine in order to improve your performance. Getting the steps right is one thing, adding the detail sets you apart from others, and I've never known any dance teacher not to answer an intelligent question about the routine. But keep questions direct and clear, not vague; there's no time for waffling.

- Remember to act throughout the routine. A good teacher or the choreographer will set the scene for you, and give character notes, helping you to discover where specific moves relate to the acting elements. Never stop acting through dance.

- Be spatially aware. This is particularly important if you're auditioning for an ensemble or swing position, where good spatial awareness is crucial. In the excitement of the moment, it's easy to forget that there are other people dancing too. Particularly with kicks or any movement backwards, where you may not be able to see who's behind you, just be careful. And if *you* are the person behind, just be conscious of what the person in front is doing and watch you don't get a mouthful of heel.

- Be generous to your fellow auditionees. While they are presenting their routine, and the routine is appropriate, encourage them. And applaud them after their routine.

- Also while watching other dancers present the routine, 'mark' the routine to yourself on the spot (i.e. go through the steps but under-energised). This will cement the routine more firmly in your head and muscle memory. But keep your marked movements subtle while you're watching. If they're too energised and big, you will distract the panel from those whose turn it is.

- It's not just about the feet. People tend to watch the face first and foremost.

- And if the feet do go wrong, just try to pick up the rest of the routine as best you can. I have seen performers give up and stomp to the side in frustration; leave frustration behind and continue as best you can.

- If the routine has been taught in sections, once performed in its entirety, aim to smooth the sections together to make a whole. Similarly allow the routine to flow. Enjoy the dramatic journey that the routine takes you on.

- If there is a moment of 'free dance' improvisation within the routine where you are given a number of bars to 'show off', keep the choreography within the style and dramatic intention of the routine. It's tempting to show off all the fabulous tricks you can do, but it's more impressive if you pick up on the style already defined by the choreographer and just show one or two spectacular but appropriate leaps, jumps or kicks. It must retain the style.

- Never change the routine you have been taught; you are not the choreographer. Instead focus on the detail you can see and replicate it.

And finally, remember that with acting and singing auditions, I can write my notes and listen to your audition without actually watching you constantly. With a dance audition I can only watch – there's no auditory benefit – and so if I'm not watching you, and my focus is on another dancer, I probably haven't spotted that little error you made. If you react to your errors, then you'll certainly pull my focus over to you. And even if we didn't miss your mistake, how you recover from a mistake is as important as if you hadn't made it in the first place. So let's not have any great dramas if you trip, or miss a step, or jump a bar earlier than everyone else. As with your songs, pretend nothing went wrong, compose yourself and pick up the rest of the routine.

The non-dancers at a dance call

If you're a non-dancer (like I was), a dance call can be a terrifying place. I used to hate them! Wearing my threadbare trainers and flabby old tracksuit bottoms it was a hideous experience walking into a room full of incredibly fit, lycra-clad chaps with their legs behind their ears and all their muscles on display.

And then to be humiliated by having to dance in front of other people. Even at weddings it was rare for me to strut my stuff. And so on several occasions I remember walking up to the likes of Gillian Lynne, Stephen Mear and Bill Deamer pleading for them to strike me off the list and make the pain go away.

At that point, I hadn't learnt this valuable lesson:

> **If you are known to be a non-dancer and you are called to a dance audition, it doesn't necessarily mean that the team are considering you for a prime dance position. It might be that they just want to see how you cope and have other plans for you within the company.**

What I'm saying here is that for most productions there will be some prime dancers, and then some secondary dancers. If there are some nice cameo roles, and you can't dance, it might be that the team love your acting enough not to worry about your lack of dance skills. You become valuable in different ways. Nonetheless, you still need to dance at some point in the show and therefore you have to go through the dance audition.

One piece of advice, for shows already running, is to see if you know anyone who's been in the show you are auditioning for and ask if they might know the audition routine and could work on it with you prior to the audition. I did this several times and it was enormously beneficial. (I still didn't get through – I was *that* bad! But at least I felt more comfortable going into the dance call.)

So the tips for non-dancers are:

- Dive into the dance audition with all your heart. You may not be as technically adept as most of the other dancers in the room, but chances are that you may be able to act and sing considerably better.

- Act through the dance. Steps are important, but if it all goes belly up (quite literally), make sure you maintain the energy and commitment of the character throughout the routine.

- Particularly use expression in your face and arms. I don't mean go wild, but keep animated. If your upper body is engaged, energised and interesting, it can take the focus away from the disaster that is happening below your waist.

- Don't give up. Stick with it. As I say, if the team already know you aren't a prime dancer, you will be there because they are considering you for other lesser dance positions within the company. But they still need to see how you hold up within a group of stronger dancers. Walking out defeated risks losing out on the rest of the audition process.

- Just because you can't dance much, don't be afraid to ask intelligent questions. It's not really acceptable for you to ask basic questions over and over, as that holds everyone up, but if you're not sure what goes where, then do ask. Most teachers will be sympathetic to your requirements.

- If you are too nervous to ask, then try to ascertain who are the strong people in the group, and then move closer to them and observe what they're doing. But don't ask them questions as they may be concentrating. If, however, they offer help, then accept it.

- Don't hide at the back of the group. You won't be able to see the teacher. Yes, of course being at the front exposes you to being totally awful, but it also shows you are trying to learn and not giving up, and that's important.

- Frequent professional dancers are used to dancing in front of a mirror, but non-dancers can find looking at themselves intimidating. You may be tempted to watch yourself, criticise yourself and then go wrong, so try not to focus on yourself, and look off slightly to one side. Although remember that for the 'showing' of the routine, you may dance away from the mirror, and so any previous reliance on seeing other helpful dancers in the mirror may be removed.

- Indeed, try not to look at other dancers and 'follow' what they do. If they make a mistake you'll be making it too, and you might not have done so if you'd kept to your convictions.

- And finally, no matter how self-conscious you may feel, enjoy it, and have fun. Dance is as much about communication as it is about the steps (although the steps and the 'physical dance line' are of course very important). If you can look as though you're having fun, or are at least committed, then we will believe you are and the effect will be beneficial for you.

Gatecrashing

If you have an agent, you will normally be given an appointment time. But sometimes your agent isn't able to get you a meeting and you have to take your own initiative. I have often been approached by lurking actors and dancers who have managed to find out where our auditions are being held and have asked whether they might be seen. While I admire anyone's efforts to be auditioned, and asking is being proactive, I have generally said that I don't have the opportunity to see them during that particular day's session, but to send their information to the office, and if appropriate, we may ask them to audition at a later date. That said, if I've had a cancellation and we are unable to fill the gap, I have been known to ask the panel if they'd like to see someone outside who has gatecrashed, and in most cases we have seen them.

But I think, on the whole, avoid gatecrashing if you can. Some casting directors take great offence to you asking. It's much better to be submitted through the proper channels, as discussed in Chapter 1. If, either via your agent or your personal approach, we still don't want to see you, it's because we don't think you're right and so turning up at an audition venue to gatecrash is going to be pretty pointless.

Open auditions

Open auditions are when any actor may turn up to audition without a specific appointment time or by pre-arrangement, and much of what we've discussed above still applies.

The general format of open auditions is as follows:

- An announcement or advert will be listed in several of the major entertainment publications giving the title of the piece, the dates, the producers and normally the type of contract you will be engaged under.

- There will be details of where to attend, and at what time.

- There may be details of whether it's a dance or singing audition and what style of song you should prepare, or what dance shoes you'll require.

- There may also be a time period during which you need to register. Registration involves handing in your CV and picture, and you may be required to complete several forms, or be allocated an audition number.

- You will be asked to stay and wait to audition, or given a specific time for later in the day.

- Once you've registered and are called into the audition room, you are likely to be auditioned in groups. If it's a singing audition, you may be asked to do a short portion of your song of less than a minute, probably unaccompanied. It's unlikely you'll sing the song in its entirety; look back at the 'sixteen-bar song' section in Chapter 2 for advice on what to do. If it's a dance call, you will probably be taught a very short routine which may just involve some technical dance elements for you to display as you travel across the room, one after the other, in eight- or sixteen-bar counts.

- Once you've performed the first audition, there is likely to be what is known as a 'cut', which is where the panel will discuss you, and then ask some people to leave. For them, it's the end of the road. For those asked to remain, it'll be likely that they have to do another dance routine, or sing a longer version of their song. There may be several rounds throughout the day, and you should be prepared to hang around all day.

- You may be asked to come back to another set of call-backs at a future point.

The open audition process should be treated in the same way as an audition set up by an agent. There's no real difference other than the speed at which open auditions take place. Because we don't necessarily know how many people may turn up, we work quickly and prefer to get an overall gauge of someone's talent, then give them more time in a call-back later on in the audition process. I once auditioned over 500 dancers in a two-hour session on *West Side Story*; it was crazy, brilliant, exciting and draining (on us as well as the auditionees). So you can understand the pace we need to work at in order to sort the wheat from the chaff.

Specific open audition tips

- For your first quick song, choose something upbeat, funny and with a great belt, lasting a minute.

- Be sure you have a range of material in your portfolio for a second song.

- Look immaculate.

- Be professional.

- Smile at the team.

- Because the pace is quick, we need to remember you at open auditions, and so on this occasion (and this occasion only) do wear something sensible that stands out.

- Also, you need fifty times as much concentration at an open call because there is a lot of waiting around, and then suddenly you have to impress in thirty seconds. Keep your energy high and listen all the time.

- Don't give off any negative attitude: '*I'm far too good to be at an open call but my lousy agent couldn't get me an audition ...*' Your agent may well have tried to nag me twenty times without any luck. So don't blame your agent. By turning up at an open call, you are being proactive. Be glad of having the opportunity to impress us.

- Don't think that no one gets cast from open auditions. They are, and indeed for some productions I've been involved with, we've found some significant company members from open calls.

- If you don't have the skills required as advertised, don't come in. I have sent people away while they've been standing in the queue outside simply because they are the wrong height, look, shape or sex (yes, I have had men turn up to open calls when we specifically announced that we'd only be casting females!).

Taped auditions

With advances in technology it's now easy to send filmed audition sessions over the internet to members of the creative team. Indeed for several shows I've cast, the auditionees never met the director until the first day of rehearsal. The entire audition process was filmed with me and other members of the creative team present, but without the director. Having shortlisted the actors, the videoed sessions were then sent to the director, and after viewing and discussing these tapes, the final cast was assembled. Live video link-up services, such as Skype, are also becoming widely used (although more for straight theatre than musicals). For a musical I was working on for Australia, I did the entire audition session on Skype with the actors, musical director and producer in Melbourne but with me in my study in north London (at three in the morning no less!). It's unusual, and we all prefer the live experience, but it will certainly become more common in future years.

When being filmed, you hardly need to do anything different from what we've already discussed. However, do ask at the audition whether you are required to look to camera or not. Some people like it, some don't.

You should also sign a 'video waiver form' from the producers stating that any footage is to be used solely for the aid of casting, must not be shown to anyone outside of the production team, will not be used for any public transmission or internet media site, and will be destroyed following the casting process.

And you're out of the room …

… you can relax. Whatever you did in the audition room is now in the past. You can't go back and improve it, and you can't make the panel think any better of you. It's all done, so relax. Try not to analyse what you did, but if you made mistakes, write them down in order to improve for next time. Fill out your audition diary. Don't beat yourself up, and don't say to yourself, *'I could have done better.'* It's too late. Instead, phone a friend and have a coffee with them. Or do some minor retail therapy (that was always my best way to let an audition go, although save the expensive items for when you get the job!). Call your agent; most agents like to know how it went.

It's not quite over yet, of course, and the most difficult bit is yet to come. The bane of an actor's life is waiting for the response to an audition. You've achieved something momentous in getting through a first round – many didn't get seen and you did, so bravo. But the wait to find out whether you have a call-back or you're going to be rejected is always stomach-churning. You can receive all the advice and support in the world. But I honestly know what that moment feels like and, however encouraging other people's words are, I know too well how agonising the wait for news, good or bad, really is. Nothing makes this process easier.

For now, be content that you did the very best audition you could.

And let's just wait for the response …

WORDS OF WISDOM

Meeting the team

Christopher Luscombe

The director hasn't got time for too much chat about your vision of the piece – if asked your opinion, give it, but avoid rambling. If you are given notes, take them – however daft they may be. It flatters the director, and shows that you're flexible. A director wants to see that you can share some fun in the rehearsal room. Be positive about the show in question, but don't get carried away. We know you want to be in it or you wouldn't be there. Crucially, don't be negative about the writing – it's unwise to audition for *Follies* and say that you're not really wild about Sondheim.

Jamie Lloyd

I'll ask you questions about the piece as a whole and your opinions of it. More importantly, I'll expect you to ask me questions about the production and what will be required of you. Have a view and don't be shy! I'll be looking for front-footed, passionate, inventive actors who are going to offer lots to the process. Don't try to second-guess what I'm looking for, and let me get to know who you really are; I want to sense what your instincts are for the role and often you will inspire me! I'm looking for a collaborator. Be brave, lift your eyes from the script and explore the text with me.

David Gilmore

Smile. The director and MD are your friends. They *want* you to be good, to be happy, to enjoy your audition and to show just what you are capable of. Trying to be over-cool can just look as if you could take it or leave it. Your enthusiasm and your personality are part of what you have on offer.

Gareth Valentine

Be friendly when you meet the panel, don't be over-loquacious, and give an impression of wanting to be in that room to perform. Never apologise for yourself.

Dominic Shaw

For anyone auditioning the most important thing, for me, is being true to who you are and not presenting something that feels false or disingenuous. Whether it's a first-round singing call or a final call-back, the audition panel wants to invest in you not just as an actor/singer/dancer but as a person, so the more of your own personality you can bring into the room the better. Leave the job of worrying whether you're right or wrong for the role to the panel, just come in fully prepared, be yourself and that's all you can ever do.

Joey McKneely

First and foremost, we *all* want you to be good ... so leave the self-doubt and self-esteem issues at the door. There are so many times I just start talking to people in the audition to see if anyone is home. It's a test ... are you listening? Can you communicate to me as a human being? Do you have fire? Are you funny? All I care about is how good you are in this moment in time. You may not get a second chance. So make the first chance count.

Remember, no matter what you see on the other side of the table...talking, eating, writing, smiles, laughs, stone faces ... do not, and I repeat, do *not* let any of that get to you. Stay focused and positive.

Some days I have seen over 500 people, haven't had lunch and am jet-lagged from arriving the day before, but I know talent when I see it ... we all do, so come in and do your best. Sometimes it's not how good your audition is ... sometimes it's about your potential.

Nerves

Gareth Valentine

Nerves will sometimes get the better of you. Breathe deep – the worst bit is waiting to enter the audition room. But if you've really done your stuff and learned your material well and thought about what every instant of every lyric means, by the time you're singing you'll be too busy and committed to the song to let nerves become an encumbrance. Take what you do seriously and it will pay dividends.

The pianist – your friend

David Gilmore

The accompanist is your ally if you treat him/her with respect. Don't make an enemy of them as you hand them your score! (Thank them on leaving regardless of how well or badly you think it went.)

Dance auditions

Dominic Shaw

With dance auditions (for musicals) it's easy to concentrate too much on the steps and forget about the purpose of the routine within the story. The choreographer will ideally explain what he or she is looking for and also give you an idea of the context of the routine. Listen very carefully to what they're trying to achieve through the movement. Good dance routines tell stories and move the piece on and enhance the piece in some way, so never approach it with the attitude that they are 'just steps'. It's just as much an acting exercise as it is a dance routine. A few wrong steps are easily forgiven as long as you're displaying the right performance quality and committing wholeheartedly to the emotion required. Another great tip is to wear something distinctive and iconic. It has to be in keeping with the style of the piece, but for the big dance calls wearing something that stands out really helps the panel remember you.

Stephen Mear

- Make sure you come fully warmed up; don't take it for granted that a warm-up will take place, as a lot of the time it doesn't; be one step ahead and well prepared.

- Keep positive; don't let yourself frown or pull faces as sometimes it can be mistaken for arrogance and even if you're hating the choreography that's being shown to you, you must make the creative team think it's the best piece you've ever done and still put everything you have into it. Charm and personality go a long way.

- Healthy competition is good; don't push to the front but make sure you are seen at least once to be near the front during the rehearsal; don't hide at the back.

- Remember you are being watched at all times, so while other groups are dancing don't chat in a corner to friends; focus and learn from previous groups and listen to all that is going on in the room and what the choreographer is looking for.

- You should show that you can focus at all times and that you are determined. If a choreographer asks you to do two pirouettes or to kick your leg to a certain height, then do exactly as they request; don't do a triple pirouette or shoulder your leg just because you can, or show off; this does not show your discipline and this is what they will be looking for.

- I was once in an audition and a group of people at the back stood bitching about people at the front. They never got picked for the jobs. It's a waste of energy to bitch about people who want to succeed and it doesn't look good on your attitude to be seen doing this. Just focus on you and what you want to achieve from the audition, not what others around you want.

- It's important to show your enjoyment for dance in the audition, whether you're getting it right or not. You can have people who have a great technique but are as dull as dishwater and have no feeling when they dance. But if you have a natural passion, determination and feel for dance but are not the best on the technique side then sometimes this will get you through to the next stage; you can teach technique but you can't teach passion. Show willingness to learn, mixed with passion and enjoyment for the dance being shown, and this will be noticed.

- If you are shown something in an audition and you genuinely need to ask something that hasn't been explained, i.e. which foot to start on, etc., then that's fine. If you're asking something unnecessary that has already been told to you, just because you want to make your presence known in the room, for the creative to remember you, then don't! We know when this is being done and it is time-wasting. You will be remembered for all the wrong reasons. Do not seek attention; just work hard and show that you are focused, determined and passionate, then you will be noticed for all the right reasons.

Bill Deamer

While I will always look for a solid dance technique in ballet, jazz and tap, it is having the ability to use that technique to dance a particular style required for a particular musical. Dancers must always embrace the specific style that a choreographer is looking for. The best example I can give is that with the constant revivals of the period musicals of the 1920s, 1930s and 1940s I would urge any dancer to study the classic Hollywood and Broadway musicals of that era and see just exactly what makes them tick. They will then see how these styles have been developed and made accessible for the Broadway and West End audiences of today. Yes, choreography has moved on but its foundations are there for us all to see. Watch, learn and understand where this is coming from. If it's a tap-dancing audition, listen to the rhythms being set and *listen to the music*! If you do 'make the cut' and are asked to sing for the musical director and the director, it is important that you have at least two appropriate songs ready to 'perform'. It is so disheartening when a choreographer loses a good dancer from the first round of auditions because they have not been prepared to sing after the dance call.

Christopher Gattelli

Ideally you have been taking class to keep up your chops, but aside from taking class to be sure your technique is up to par, it is also helpful in preparing your brain to pick up combinations. I can tell from auditions who has and hasn't been in class by the way people pick up a combination. If they pick it up quickly and notice the details, you can tell their brain is used to steps and style being thrown out to them regularly.

I personally watch and take note of people from the second they walk in the room. Their confidence, how they are treating other dancers around them, and what they are wearing and if it is appropriate for that show. No matter what people say – '*Oh, they're creative. They can picture us in the costumes*' – we are, yes, but honestly, every little bit helps. I'm not saying come dressed up in sequins and feathers, but something that is appropriate to the style of the show definitely helps. It at least shows me you've done your homework and know what the show is about.

The main thing when learning the combination is listen to the person (normally the choreographer) teaching the combination. *Really* listen. It's not just about the steps and hitting that turn ... listen past the steps being taught and hear what that character is supposed to be feeling, doing, thinking. It's all in those little details that will set someone apart for me. Of course you have to dance your best, but I always feel that as long as you have the brains behind the technique, that is what seals the deal. I can clean you up and perfect things in weeks of a rehearsal process, that's what they are for ... but take risks in an audition. Don't settle on what you think is safe for you or you'll fall back into your comfort zone, and I can always see that behind the eyes. Really be in the dance, be present, when you are performing it. If you are, we can tell and it won't matter if you hop on a turn, or hobble on a step.

Non-dancers

Christopher Gattelli

And for those who would consider themselves a 'non-dancer', you have to know you can dance. Everyone can dance. I believe that. Most of the time I see people who don't consider themselves a dancer not do well, mainly because they get self-conscious and get nervous. So then it becomes a knock-on effect. They get nervous, so they can't focus, and then can't pick up the combination, etc. The main thing that will help this is to find a class that you feel comfortable taking and go as often as you can, if only just so that you can feel comfortable dancing in a room with other people, and learn how to pick up a combination. It doesn't even matter how simple the class is. Just that you are going is a huge step. You can then walk in the audition feeling that you have those lessons under your belt. I know that you can do it. If something is a bit too difficult for you, honestly, just do your best, and do it with confidence. Not everyone can do everything. Like singing, not everyone can hit a high C. That doesn't mean that if someone can't they are not a good singer. Find your strengths, and embrace your strengths. But don't compensate and try to over-dance. Again, if you have been listening, you will hear what we want as we teach. Again, you just have to show us that you can pick up and perform it with confidence no matter what level your technique is.

5

CALL-BACKS AND BEYOND

You sit there looking at your phone, willing it to ring. Five days have passed since your audition. Nothing. You thought you'd done all right, and went out and bought that new top as a present to yourself for doing so well. Just as you begin to wonder what lunch you can afford before going overdrawn on your bank card, the phone rings. You grab it as if it's the first time you've ever heard it ring.

'Hello, darling?'

'Dorothy? Hi ... *(breath)* ... how's things?'

'Well, about to get a lot better, sweetheart, I hope. You've got a call-back. Write this down ...'

A little skip by the phone and you grab for your pencil and audition diary.

'So, Tuesday. The Stable Studios, 3 p.m. Take the same songs – they loved them. They're also going to send you some music and text from the show. They want to see you for Frankie, who also covers the lead, Bernie. Both great roles. Now you're going to do a dance call first. Don't stress; it's not difficult, apparently. Then you'll do your scene work and songs. They want you to change your look ...' and so Dorothy continues her list of things you need to work on.

Call-backs

Getting a call-back is fantastic news, but it means there's still work to do. Knowing you got through the first stage is wonderful news; yes, you beat some others, but it's not all plain sailing yet. You still have competition, and from now on, everyone else is also feeling the pressure and raising their game. So must you.

A call-back may come days after your first audition, but in most professional productions it could be weeks, possibly months, later; it's likely that there may be several call-backs over the audition process.

Essentially, the skills we've already discussed about auditioning in previous chapters are the same for call-backs. But key things to remember are:

- If we call you in again to audition, it's because we see some further potential in you, which we want to explore. This is a positive sign, so you too must be positive. The stakes are higher, but so are your chances of landing the role.

- Because we want to explore you again, you need to be more knowledgeable about the project and character, and then be able to apply that information in order to play the director's intentions accurately.

- Wear the same clothes and keep the same look – unless, of course, you are specifically asked to change it. It worked for you the first time and a change of look may be counter-productive.

- Always take your original song choices, plus additional songs to show your full range, as well as any new material you are given. So many people forget to take their music book to call-backs and suddenly get caught out when we ask for something different. And the excuse 'I've only got this one song with me' suggests laziness and lack of interest.

- If – and it's possible – you are joining the audition

process at the call-back stage (without any first round), you must work harder still. Most other people will have already had a sense of the production, will have met at least some of the creative team, and possibly have already presented material from the production and have previously been directed on it. You have to be as good as, if not better than, them, despite this being your first audition.

New members of the panel

Over the course of the call-backs, various members of the creative and production team will join the audition panel. This may mean that you won't necessarily present anything new at your audition, just repeat material you've done previously. Try hard to maintain those initial instincts and energy that got you through the previous auditions; I once got feedback (having been rejected) that I had lost my spontaneity over the course of the lengthy audition process – I had become 'stale' in my approach to the material and it no longer felt fresh and exciting. You can't ever let this happen. Each new member of the panel will be seeing you for the first time, and just as you would in performance, your audition for them must be as exciting as the first time you auditioned.

New material

By the call-back stage, we are likely to have decided which character we think most fits you and will send you music from the show together with some scene text (also called 'sides'). Having done your research on the show for the initial audition round, you should already be familiar with the piece, and thereby the characters. So first, go back to your original notes on the piece and work out what your character does within the show.

The most important points about new production material are:

> **For call-backs you must learn both music and text by heart. You must gather your background information in order to deliver a truthful character in context of the piece.**

So many actors don't bother to learn their material thoroughly and then wonder why they do poor call-backs. The preparation of show-specific material, and the homework you do on that material, is as important, if not more, than the preparation you had to do for your first meeting. You will normally be given material to prepare and learn at least a few days in advance of your call-back. Sometimes, for practical reasons, it isn't possible to do this, but even in twenty-four hours, try to do your very best to learn the material as best you can. In truth, it isn't going to be disastrous if you have to hold your script, but trust me, without it you will be freer in your interpretation and present the material without worrying about what's coming next. The worst scenario is, of course, when we've sent the script out well in advance, and it looks as if someone has only seen it for the first time. It really is a waste of everyone's time.

Text work

With the text you've been sent, you need to make similar choices to your scenes as you do with your songs.

To start off, ask yourself general questions about the character:

- What are the character's key personality traits?

- What is the character's function within the story?

- What are the key moments for your character within the show?

- With whom does the character associate?

- What are the character's downfalls?

- What are the character's successes?

- What do other characters say about your character?

You can, I'm sure, think of many more questions, and questioning your character at this point provides vital intelligence to this next stage of the audition process. Knowing who your character is and what (s)he does in the musical will provide you with a greater understanding of how to deliver the role convincingly in an audition situation. Even if you are auditioning for an ensemble character, whose qualities are not specifically defined by the authors, you still need to identify key elements as to how you might play the character. The advantage with an ensemble character is that you can invent some of the information, whereas with a more detailed named role, there will be character information already provided in the script.

- Next, read through the scene. Ask yourself what the situation is – is the scene generally about love? Heartbreak? Humour? Sadness? Anger? Happiness? What is the character's journey – how does it start, how does it finish and how did it change within the scene? Which role is more dominant? Which character is weaker? Does this change?

- Define where the climax of the scene is, and then define the pace and momentum of the scene around that climax.

- Go further into defining what is being said. Are the characters open with their speech – are they telling the truth or are they lying? Is their true intention not actually what they're saying?

- And finally break down the sentences – why has the author used certain words? What do they tell you about the character's intelligence, intentions, background, etc.? Why are they saying what they're saying at this point in the musical?

- And, as ever in acting, listen to what the other character is saying. Truthful acting is all about listening and responding, the same as in real life. We talk, someone listens and replies, we listen and respond. Don't, as so many do in auditions, just focus on your own lines. So many people 'shut down' when the other character speaks; it's un-engaging and, of course, not what anyone expects of a talented performer.

There are a lot of questions to ask, but by finding answers and thereby making acting choices, you read with intelligence rather than providing just a surface-level reading with little thought behind it. The key thing to remember, though, is once you've made your choices, don't let them become so ingrained in your mind that you can't change them if asked. The director may not like your interpretation and will expect you to be prepared to play with the role and try it in different ways.

Be brave

So many call-back auditionees I see are unfortunately less good than when we first saw them. Perhaps it's due to the extra pressure, the learning of new material, or many other reasons which get in the way, causing auditionees to deliver performances which often make us wonder what we saw in them in the first place. Try not to let any distractions cloud your judgement at a call-back. Be positive and look forward to enjoying the experience of auditioning in greater detail. Step up to the mark and, above all, be brave. Of course, keep within the parameters that have been set by the director's explanation of the role, and of what you know of the piece, but be brave enough to take that direction and then have fun discovering how far you can go with the material. As previously mentioned, it's much easier for a director to rein in a performance if it's a little 'too much' than it is to have to coax a performance out of you. Keep truthful, of course, and importantly, keep within the style of the material, but with your background knowledge to hand, take the challenging options rather than going for the obvious choices.

Asking questions

At the risk of being reprimanded, I often find that many directors don't convey what they want at auditions, and expect an actor just to 'find it'. Sometimes, too, directors think that actors can only perform scenes one particular way and don't give them an opportunity to try another approach. It's true that part of what we're looking for is a natural, instinctive approach to a role and one individual's response is very different from another's. But nonetheless, actors act; they are experienced in showing a range of characters and so, with guidance and notes, decent actors can change the nuances of a character and play it any number of ways.

I'm staggered how many times an actor has left the room and the director has said, 'Well, it's not what I wanted,' without having actually *said* what they wanted from the actor while they were still in the room. How are you, as the actor (or indeed I as the casting director) supposed to know what's in the director's head if they don't tell us? On many of those occasions, and particularly when I've known the skill base of the actor concerned, I've simply called the actor back in and asked the director to explain what it is they were seeking from the actor. Lo and behold, now armed with this new knowledge, in most cases the actor can play the director's new intention brilliantly!

At call-backs I would urge you to ask your director questions, both in terms of your text work and song work. Some directors are very good at describing what they want, and similarly it's a casting director's job to relay those intentions to the actor in advance. I had several moments in my acting career where a director's vision of a role had changed during the audition process but this wasn't relayed to me, and I therefore spent subsequent call-backs going over the same (and now wrong) approach to the character.

It's your job to ask questions such as '*Is that how you wanted it?*' or '*Would you like it a little more anxious / frustrated/ charming / angry/ sexual/ etc. etc.?*' If you think you may have gone a little too far in the audition, then ask the director. '*I don't think I got that, did I? Can I try again, a little calmer perhaps...?*' etc. are permissible questions at call-backs, and will probably elicit a greater response from the director to give you even more guidance as to their interpretation of the character. It's your opportunity to make your mark and it's up to you to find the director's intentions for the role, however vague they may be at this stage. By asking questions, and taking on board the responses that are given, you may also unlock a new and exciting performance from yourself, and give us a new perception as to how the character might be played, as well as a new approach to you as a performer. Remember, though, that it's better to be showing off your talent through the scene-work than talking about it. Two or three questions at the most, and then get on with the scene.

Looking at you in a new way

It's sometimes the case that during this more detailed call-back work on the material, we discover something new in your performance which results in the decision that you would be better moved to a different character than the one you originally were suggested for. In many cases, this is a good thing, as it could mean we are struggling to find someone to play that new role, and by accident we've discovered that you are the one we were looking for all along. That can be very exciting for all of us. If, however, you are asked to change to another role, you shouldn't feel rushed into working on new material. Ask if you can have a few days to prepare it and get a later audition time, rather than rushing through it on the spot.

Readers

In the same way as the pianist is there to aid you in your song, so the reader is there to 'accompany' you in your dialogue. In my auditions, I will tend to read with you directly because I like knowing how you listen and respond. I also know what the director wants, so my dialogue with you will normally lead you in the direction we want. Some directors like to read with you themselves. There have been several directors who purposely read with a 'flatness' in order for you to work harder, or present you with obstacles to see how you overcome them. Personally I don't see the point in this; it's much easier for you to play against a reader who responds to you with expression so that you can invest fully in the scene. But beware – there are some awful readers out there. At worst, you may get someone with no acting skill whatsoever who simply delivers the lines in a monotonous dirge. Try your best to maintain as truthful and characterful a performance as you can and don't worry about how bad they are. This is your audition, not theirs, and you must also take control of the scene-work as best you can. In the same way as the panel will make allowances for a poor pianist, so they will for a poor reader.

Accents

Unless you've been told to do a specific accent, or it is explicit in the text, make sensible choices about the character's accent. Ask yourself where the piece is set, what class the character is, and what situation they are in, all of which will change their accent. If you're unsure, call the casting office. And prepare the script in two ways – one with an accent you feel works and one with your own natural accent. In terms of stereotypical character voices, or spoken afflictions such as a lisps, stammers, pronouncing 'w' instead of 'r', etc., avoid them all unless you know they are specifically required.

Should I stand up for text work?

Some directors like you seated at the casting table, some like you to stand. Ask what the preference is. Either way, you need to give energy and commitment to your scene, whether you're standing or sitting. You should never hide or mumble behind your script (which you don't need anyway because you've learnt it, right?).

Where's my eyeline during text work?

Personally, I believe that you should make contact with the reader, wherever they are. If the reader is behind the casting table, then play to them. If the reader is up on a stage with you, then again play to them but ensure that you don't spend too much time in profile and side-on as you speak to them. It's likely that the reader will be fairly static, and may unintentionally upstage you. Be sure that the panel can see you clearly. Find the dramatic moments within the speech to cross the stage or face out into the auditorium.

Should I move around?

As with your song, be careful not to include too much unnecessary movement within your scene-work. It'll be distracting. If you are standing with a reader – and of course the reader won't know what blocking (movement) you have thought about – then make one or two natural moves throughout the scene. And if you need a chair, then yes, use one. But keep movement to key dramatic moments where a move feels natural and emotionally appropriate.

Dealing with poor text

I'm sorry to say that not all musical theatre dialogue is award-winning. A fair proportion of it is truly dire, whether new or old-fashioned. Nevertheless, you must invest in your dialogue with utter conviction and truth. No matter how awful the words you have to say, please treat them with respect. Often musical theatre scene-writing is poor because it goes for the obvious or cliché line rather than being truly inventive. Often the text may be rushed and fail to provide significant character reference or plot development, functioning merely as a way of getting from one song to the next. Where possible, try not to highlight these faults and instead give the text a fresh meaning or interpretation. It's not your fault that it's bad writing, but it is your fault if you don't do something to hide the fact that it's bad, and instead choose to make your character (and by default, you) look and sound completely ridiculous. Conviction, truth and inventive interpretation – they are the keys to making poor dialogue a little better.

Reading at sight

If you are asked to read at sight – i.e. immediately in the audition room – first ask if you may go outside with the text to read it over while the next auditionee comes in. Most directors will say yes. Of course it's impossible for you to prepare newly given text in the same way as if you'd had it in advance. Whether you are allowed time out of the room or not:

- Take a few moments to skim the text.

- Get an overall sense of the scene and what the pace of the scene is.

- Get a sense of the character's overall intention, purpose in the scene, mood and accent and a general feel of their status.

- Read any difficult words or names several times so they become familiar to you.

And then dive in. It's likely that the director will give you direction and you'll get another go at it. If you fluff some lines it's OK. Correct yourself and carry on. If you make a real mess, it's perfectly acceptable on a 'cold reading' to ask to go back to the beginning.

Dyslexia

If you are dyslexic, make sure your agent is aware of it, and ask for the scripts, music and sides to be sent out well in advance. There is absolutely nothing to be ashamed of if you have trouble reading – indeed many brilliant (and famous) actors suffer from dyslexia and similar conditions. But it's vitally important for the casting director to know that you may not be able to sight-read and he should give you a call-back at a later point, giving you more time to study the text. I have twice rejected actors for what I believed to be bad readings, only to be told afterwards by the agents at the feedback stage that the actors were dyslexic. All too late at that point, as we had made offers to other actors. I repeat, there is nothing to be ashamed of, nor will it disadvantage you in terms of finally landing the role. Just be sure that someone on the casting team knows so that we can take the appropriate steps to support you and give you the very best opportunity to display your talent.

Call-back songs

You should treat your call-back songs in the same way as you did your own songs. Look back over those early chapters to remind yourself of the techniques and questions we employed to improve your knowledge and understanding of what the song demands. Ask lots of questions about character, and look at the lyrics carefully; find out what they mean, what the lyricist is trying to achieve by using certain words. And again, learn all your material thoroughly.

Should I see the show I'm auditioning for at a call-back stage?

If you are auditioning for an existing production, then I urge you to see the production as soon as you can. If you are several call-backs into the audition and you haven't seen it, then ask the casting office if they can arrange a ticket for you. It's highly unlikely that the ticket will be complimentary, but you may be able to get a company-rate ticket at a reduced price.

By seeing the production you will immediately get a sense of the style of the production. Try to keep an eye specifically on the character you are auditioning for, even if they are not necessarily the central focus all the time. Remember, this is not a fun night out at the theatre – it's for you to study the role in question carefully (although ideally that in itself will be an enjoyable exercise). Also, see if there's a sound recording of this production. That will help.

If you are not able to see a production live, then see if there are any on-line recordings. Web clips become incredibly useful, if only to give you a sense of style and character, although use these only as a guide as they may not represent the production you are auditioning for.

Should I copy the performance I see or hear?

In general, no, you shouldn't copy someone else's performance. Obviously in a long-running musical there are elements of performance that inevitably are required to remain the same. But if you can bring something appropriately unique to the role in keeping with the intentions of the production, that excites us at the audition stage. Of course, some productions may simply want a carbon copy of what is already being portrayed on stage, and you will have to discover if that is required by asking the casting director or director. I was in a number of productions where a well-meaning resident director explained at auditions that there would be the opportunity to 'take the role in a new direction' should I get it. Yet, having signed the contract, I discovered that 'my new interpretation' would ultimately be left within the walls of my dressing room and the resulting performance was essentially required to be the same as it had been previously played by a generation of actors.

Keeping on top of your call-back

It's highly likely that for a professional musical, particularly a new musical, there will be more than one call-back. I once had over fifteen call-backs for one role!

Some tips to remember:

- Always keep on top of the audition material. So long as you know you're still in the running for the role, you should regularly remind yourself of the material, and when you go revisit it, see if you can discover something distinctive that might bring renewed energy to the scene.

- At the end of each audition, once out of the room, write down the notes that you received from the director. There are many auditions where an actor comes in for the third or fourth time, having forgotten what we said in the previous auditions, and therefore takes back-steps. It's frustrating having to repeat direction notes and shows a lack of care and attention on your part. Every minute we have to repeat ourselves is a minute less that you have to show us something new and wonderful.

- It may be a few weeks between each call-back but you must go into each with the same commitment and zest that you did on that first audition day. It's tough to keep repeating the same material to a lifeless panel, but just as you would in performance, you must keep the material exciting, new and spontaneous for each call-back you attend. We keep calling you in because we're still interested in you and want you to do well. Don't let us down.

- Obtain feedback from the casting director throughout the audition process. If you are being called back time and time again, find out from the casting director how you can improve on your performance. What might give you the edge and what might be letting you down?

- Enjoy every second of the call-backs. You're still in the frame, and you are closer to being cast. Of course this carries with it increasing pressure, but remain professional, dedicated and alert, do your homework and do your best. That's all you can do.

Why are there so many call-backs in which I keep doing the same thing?

I know it can be frustrating, time-consuming and often costly to come in for multiple call-backs. Believe me, if we could cast a production in one call-back, then we would; we really wouldn't bother calling you in if we didn't like you and want to explore further possibilities with you.

There are many reasons why we may need to keep calling you back, and a few of the more likely are:

- As the process starts to define who we really like, and possibly new contenders come into the frame, we need to be reminded of what you bring to the table, particularly if the process takes place over many weeks or months.

- Not all the creative team who need to see you are available on the same day. The availability of important creatives, producers and others is hugely complex and sometimes difficult to schedule all on the same day.

- A change in the direction of the piece or characters dictates that we need to see if you can play the new interpretation.

- We are having a difficult choice to make between you and several other contenders, and need to see you again and explore your talent further.

- There is disagreement between the panel about you. It's often easier to solve such a dispute by calling you in again.

- We may have offered the role to someone who has turned it down and we don't have an alternative.

Group auditions

Some directors like to pair actors up for call-backs and this may mean that you are called for a longer audition until all the combinations of performers are seen. Obviously finding the right combination of people who work well together is important. If you find yourself auditioning within a group audition, then show a sense of generosity. You are auditioning together (rather than you with a reader) and that means you have to play off each other effectively and intuitively. It demands additional concentration, and sharing the audition experience. As with a reader, you won't know what blocking the other actor has decided on, but given that you must now share the scene, you must also be generous of spirit and open-handed in respecting each other's approach to the material. Have fun playing opposite your fellow auditionee.

I remember one audition where I spent a whole day reading one role against thirty or so different girls who were reading for the other character in the scene. As the day progressed, I began to believe the job was mine. Except that at the end of the day, the director kindly informed me that while all my work that day had been 'admirable', they had already cast the role I'd been reading for. It had gone to a TV actor, but he was filming and unavailable for this day of call-backs. I had been second choice!

The final audition

You will almost certainly know it's the final audition in the process when you see a lot of 'suits' on the panel. These are likely to be the money men (the producers), and you will probably have to present all the material you have been given over the entire audition process for the final time. At this audition there might be over ten people on the auditioning panel, and that can be intimidating. Just keep remembering everything you've already been taught by the previous auditions, and that you have only one opportunity for this new audience to get excited by your talents.

Often in these final auditions, this is the one audition that can make all the difference. All those earlier call-backs have, in effect, been the preparation for this final audition and you must 'up your game' and put everything you have into doing the very best you can. At this stage, everyone has gathered together to see the best people to be considered for each role. There will be several members of the panel (the casting director, the director, the musical director and the choreographer) who have gone on the audition journey with you, meeting with you each time and working with you to refine your auditions and response to the character. But these new important people, in seeing you for the first time, will make their decision based purely on what they see today, without knowing any history. Truly, no one individual will make the casting decision (it's always a collaborative process, although certain members of the team will have a stronger say than others) and also in the various discussions about you, those who have seen you previously will certainly bring to the discussion all the positive comments on your previous auditions. But don't underestimate how important this final audition is. This is it – the last opportunity to show how fabulous you are. It all boils down to this final moment. Relish it, sail through it and give it your all.

The end of the audition process

At the end of this final audition, thank everyone for seeing you, and if it's been a particularly long audition process, on this occasion it is permissible to shake the hands of the director and members of the team you've worked with most over the course of your auditions. Being something of an emotional fellow, I have been known to get a little teary at the end of a long audition process. It's an emotional journey for the team as well and like you, we have invested a great deal of time and energy in making sure the process is as thorough, professional and enjoyable as possible. Coming to the end of the audition process is momentous for everyone.

For us, now, we have to make the exciting, although intricate, decisions about how to put our company together.

For you, that's it. Back to the waiting game. Of course, the further you are along the process, the more agonising the wait now is. It could be weeks before you get a call – if indeed you get one at all. I'm afraid some casting directors and managements feel that despite you coming in a number of times it's acceptable for them not to tell you the outcome.

As before, the best piece of advice I can give, difficult though it is to follow, is to forget about it all. There's nothing more you can now do to influence the outcome.

The decision-making process

I often get asked what happens in the hours and days after the final auditions have taken place. Of course, it's totally different every time we cast a project – the decision-making process can be very quick or it can be long and drawn out. But here are some of the common situations that occur, which I hope give you some understanding.

Normally, after the final auditions, all the key members of the artistic team (director, musical director, choreographer, producers, casting directors, etc.) will convene and discuss everyone who has made it through to the final calls. In the main, there will be three groups of people: those who can now be taken through to final discussion, those who are borderline (i.e. we like them, but they don't quite offer enough to be front runners) and those who can now be rejected. However, we may not release anyone just yet in case we need to revisit them.

All the CVs of those to be discussed will be laid out in their corresponding roles and the discussion begins. Some roles are very easily decided upon; there will be clear favourites, or there may only be one choice left to us and that's that.

With other roles, it may not be so simple, and we begin to weigh up lots of possibilities, and this can often come down to very small details, many of which could be personal (your height, your look, the tone of your voice, etc.) and less about your talent (given that by this point we hope to include you as one of our great top choices). Remember, we may have taken a number of people on the journey with us, but now, as the company forms, it might be that you're simply an inch too tall to play opposite another actor. Or your energy isn't quite right. Or, taking all your auditions into account, your progress didn't quite live up to the potential we felt you had previously. Up to now, it's pretty much been about you as an individual; do you have what we're looking for artistically for the particular role? Now, all that changes; we're putting a company together, and how you fit within a company is a major consideration and factored into the final decision. Good casting is not only about having talented actors in the show, but also about putting together a company of actors who work as a team; who complement the company as a whole single entity.

When casting ensemble roles, we are also looking for someone who delivers a wide range of other attributes. An actor who offers a number of understudy possibilities becomes very useful, as does someone who has a wide range of specialist skills, such as acrobatics or a musical instrument. Or someone who offers various swing possibilities, or is renowned for being a reliable dance captain. Additionally, there is often a fair amount of swapping around.

Once everyone on the audition team has had their say, it may be that the show track which we had originally thought of you for no longer works, and we move you to another role. In one recent audition process, a particular actor who provided us with many possibilities was placed in six or seven performance tracks before we finally settled on the one that was offered. Can you see now why showing us as many facets of your talent as possible is so important in an audition? We may not have auditioned you for every possible outcome, but having seen your range, we feel confident that by placing you in a certain position you'll do a superb job.

Sometimes, having now found someone who we consider to be a better fit than you, we may decide to place you in the understudy position of the role you auditioned for. Of course, we do understand that an understudy may not necessarily be right for you at this time in your career, but that doesn't stop us from asking. Normally in a post-audition discussion, casting directors will have a fairly sound judgement about whether you will or won't take a certain level of role, although we will also ask your agent before any decisions are made.

Discussions can get very tense, often resulting in everyone having a break and 'sleeping' on the difficult decisions. And as I said at the beginning of this book, part of my job is to mediate these discussions. A director may want the best actor, but the music department feels that their voice isn't quite right, the choreographer feels they have two left feet and the producers don't think they're famous enough. It's very much about honest, frank negotiation between all departments and, more often than not, there is some degree of compromise from one department to another.

Profile casting

I often get asked my opinion about profile casting – i.e. when an actor with varying degrees of 'fame' gets cast in a production.

First, I think it's important to say that musical productions are incredibly expensive to put on and producers are obviously keen to maximise the return they get on ticket sales. Who wouldn't be? If you put several million into funding a production, you'd want to see that money back, right? Some producers believe that the quality of their production is sufficient to win over the audience and create great sales without any famous names in the cast. Others prefer to cast 'star' actors in leading roles, feeling that if the audience sees a few famous faces/names on the posters and leaflets, and then on stage, it will attract them into buying tickets.

And for many non-star actors that's a problem – often I hear comments that an actor from a major TV soap isn't as good as a particular non-profiled actor. Or that the producers are 'selling out' by casting a faded reality-TV star. It's true that sometimes an artist is cast because of their media profile instead of their artistic ability, and I have been accused on several occasions of doing exactly that.

But, at the end of the day, if a producer feels the need to cast a profile artist and that production gets produced as a result, then surely this is better than the production being cancelled and other actors remaining unemployed. Of course, any good casting director aims to ensure that profile casting is also of a high artistic quality, delivering both box-office cachet and artistic excellence. One of the proudest moments of my career to date was casting Patrick Swayze in *Guys and Dolls* in London – he was both a box-office draw and a complete joy in the role of Nathan Detroit. It's not always easy to achieve this goal, and one has to remember that the producers are our bosses and expect us to do what they want. But we certainly spend a excessive amount of time trying to please the marketing, press and production departments as well as serve the artistic demands of the production.

As 'unfair' as profile casting may seem to some, casting famous people in the leading roles has been around for years and years; it's not a new phenomenon and will always be of key importance for some producers. It may mean that you have been auditioning for a role that then goes to someone famous. It happened to me three times and I know you will feel frustrated and perhaps even a little angry in the knowledge that you may have done a better job.

My advice to you is try not to get flustered by losing out due to star casting. There's nothing you can do about it other than grit your teeth and move on. Relish the time when your career moves in the right direction, providing you with a profile of your own. Look forward to the day when we can cast you as the famous name in the hot new musical with your name above the title.

Approvals

At the end of the discussions, we have our first cast (the cast we intend to offer to) and then several back-ups for each role in case the first offer is not accepted. We then may have to get this company approved by a variety of other people such as writers (who may not have been on the panel), writers' estates (the people who look after the works of authors and composers who are deceased), co-producers, originating producers and others. This can often take time and may present further discussion in the event they don't agree with the rest of the creative and production teams.

Finally, we can go to the agents and inform them of our decision.

Rejection

No matter how fabulously talented you are, no matter what tips and hints you've learnt through this book, and no matter how hard you work, rejection is – I'm afraid – the worst and most upsetting part of this business. It's wretched, but the fact is you will certainly be rejected more times than you land roles. Out of those thousands of submissions we had at the beginning of the audition process, it was inevitable from the outset that only one person could land each role. It may be that you're incredibly talented, but ultimately you may simply not be right. No matter how good you are, you can never know exactly what's in the heads of the creative teams and what other factors may inform the final decision-making process. You will be upset, you will cry, you will be frustrated or angry and you will be disappointed.

There are three key things to remember, which I hope will make you feel a little better if you get rejected.

Once you've been to several call-backs, the final
decision will be much less about your talent and
much more about whether you fit in the company.
That is out of your control.

Second,

You were given a wonderful opportunity.
If you can honestly say you worked hard and did the
very best you could, then you should be enormously
proud of yourself.

Don't underestimate what you have achieved. At best you've
improved your skills, met new creative teams, shown you have
immense talent and proved that you are worthy of being called
an actor. If you haven't done your best, then at least you have
learnt valuable lessons upon which you can improve for the
next round of auditions.

And third,

Don't think a rejection is the end of the road – in
terms of that particular role it is, yes – but to have
got down to the final audition stages means you have
impressed the team greatly and they will certainly
want to see you again for future projects.

I touched on this earlier in the book, but it's more relevant
now in relation to discussions about how to handle rejection.
If you've given the very best you can, and you've been close

to getting the roles, I promise that you will be remembered for the future. I've known numerous situations where actors have been rejected for one project only to have been brought in by the same casting director for another production a week later and to get an offer. Everything has its purpose and so long as you work hard and you have the talent, then I promise you that one day the reward will be yours.

Feedback

If you've been to several call-backs, and then been rejected, most casting directors will be happy to provide feedback. Most of it will be constructive and helpful for you next time you audition, so learn from the criticism and see where you can improve. You may not agree with some of it or it may be difficult to accept. It is still valuable, even if difficult to hear, as it represents the honest perceptions of how you come across in the audition room. If you can learn from the feedback, then do so and work harder ready for the next audition.

Sometimes, the feedback may be that the role just didn't go your way and there is no real constructive advice to be given. Be heartened by this – it means you're doing well, but due to all those additional factors, it's not your time this time.

And if you're regularly getting close, down to the last few choices for each role, but never quite getting there, then have a heart-to-heart with your agent. They'll be able to give you good advice and encouragement and will find out a little more detail about why it's not quite happening for you from the casting directors. Some casting directors may also be happy to speak to you directly.

Of course, it's not always rejection, is it … ?

WORDS OF WISDOM

Call-backs

Vanessa Scammell
Leave the room knowing you have given yourself every chance to succeed. And if, as happens in the crazy world of casting, you're simply not the right look, height or even age, make your mark. You'll be top o' the list next time.

Bill Deamer
Casting is such a crucial and personal part of the production process and when casting dancers, I always ask the questions 'Do I want this person to become part of my team, part of the production and part of my life for the next year or so?' Let's dance and find out.

Final thoughts

Richard Eyre
In the end – beyond the ability to sing and dance and act and have stamina and be a collaborative member of a company – it's the taste of the jury (or its strongest members) that counts. And by definition that's indefinable, subjective and, to the rejected,

always unjust. As in life, the only way to audition successfully is to be honest and to be true to yourself and your abilities; in short, to act in good faith.

Christopher Luscombe
Of course a successful audition will also depend on factors beyond your control. Height, age, weight – you can't do much about those (well, not overnight anyway). So don't get too steamed up. You can only do your best.

Jerry Mitchell
My best advice, words of wisdom, encouraging thoughts to all auditioning and going through the casting process is to be true to yourself and give completely in every audition. You're not in competition with the person who went in before you or will come after. You're in competition with yourself; to be the very best you can be. If it's a match, it is a match. If it's not, then so be it. Your job is to audition every day as often as you can and always bring the four Ds (Desire, Drive, Discipline and Dedication) with you as you build your career in theatre.

Gareth Valentine
Not getting through auditions is part of the rough and tumble of showbusiness. Don't be despondent. Often you will not get through because you simply didn't fit into an often exhaustive list of criteria from voice type, look, height and almost any idiosyncrasy you can imagine. Your attitude must be to press on and only, *only* with hard application and a keen understanding of your text and an ability to serve it well will you make sure headway. Good luck.

Christopher Gattelli

For me this is the most important thing: if you have prepared as much as you can, and you have done your best, embrace that and leave it in the room. Meaning, don't go home and worry about call-backs, getting the job, etc. When I was a performer there were times when I thought I gave a great audition and was confident I would get a job, and didn't, and plenty of auditions when I didn't do my best, but got the job regardless. I say that because there is so much that goes into casting someone that you have no control over. I see it now all the time and wish I had known that as a performer. So if you don't get something, be honest with yourself and ask *'Did I really do my best? Was I prepared?'* If you feel that they are 'yes' answers, then keep doing what you are doing. Just keep working as hard as you can, and do it because you love it. Know that when you walk in the room, we want you to get the job. We want you to make our job easier by being great so we can use you.

Joey McKneely

Let me leave you with this ... I learnt how to audition by going to every audition and watching and dancing my butt off every time. I remember I got cut from an audition in LA once, but the choreographer told me she loved my dancing. The next year she remembered me when I auditioned for her for another show. Her name was Arlene Phillips. And she hired me for my very first Broadway show. See, you never know when the moment will arrive. This is why you make every moment count!

6

FINAL THOUGHTS

'Hello ?'
'Darling. It's me, Dorothy.'
'Yes …'
'Are you sitting down?'
'Yes …'
'Well, you'd better get that Press Night outfit cleaned. You got the job!'

Of course there's still the deal to negotiate, contracts to sign, partners to talk to, particularly if you're now going to be on tour for a year. But it's the best feeling in the world to receive an offer. Enjoy the moment. It's a great feeling, and congratulations.

In closing, I hope that this book has helped you, and continues to help you in your future auditions. I hope too that you have gained some insight into the process of casting. As I said at the beginning, every process is different and every casting director's approach is too. Every audition will be unique and every audition panel will throw new challenges at you. I hope, however, that I have given you some understanding of how it all works for me and many others, and these skills will benefit you in your own understanding of the audition process, and help you to obtain your goals and ambitions.

Most of all, remember;

- *Prepare. Prepare. Prepare.* I cannot say this enough!

- *Never stop learning, discovering and working hard with a view to always giving your best.* You cannot afford to busk your way through our business and working hard is the only way to succeed – whether that's through your preparation or your performance. Giving your very best at every opportunity is vitally important.

- *Believe in yourself.* You'll find that alongside all the wonderful aspects of our business, and there are many, it can often be very lonely and there will certainly be those who try to put you down. So you must believe in yourself and have confidence in your talent. You already know that landing a role isn't just about talent; there are many factors. But being confident and assured has a huge effect on your performance. You don't need to flaunt your confidence, or talk about yourself all the time, about how fabulous you are. Just remind yourself how good you are, every now and then, quietly to yourself.

And the most important thing to remember is:

- *Enjoy yourself.* Auditions don't need to be terrifying, and if you've done the work as outlined within these pages, you can go to any audition with confidence and energy, looking forward to the experience that lies ahead. One little secret is that the aim is not about landing the job, it's about getting to the next stage. Getting the job is just the pay-off for all the fun you have in auditions. So each time you enter the room, see it as a new exciting challenge, with a group of people who want to play along with you and want to get the very best out of you.

Now, go out there and audition brilliantly. I wish you the best of luck and hope to see you auditioning with me some day.

GLOSSARY

a cappella	without accompaniment
accompanist	the pianist playing the piano or keyboard
agent	the person who works with an actor to obtain auditions, and manage and negotiate your career as an actor
audition material	the script or song you are asked to prepare
back-catalogue shows	musicals with music taken from popular chart music
back-phrase	delaying the melody by not maintaining the strict musical timing
ballad	a slow sentimental or romantic song
blocking	the physical staging of a scene
book	the script of a musical
breakdown	the detailed description of the characters within a production and the requirements of the actors being submitted for consideration. Sent out to agents and artists by the casting director
call	a rehearsal, audition, performance or workshop
call-backs	being asked to audition again for the same production following your first audition. Also called recalls

casting breakdown	the detailed casting requirements of a production
Choreographer	the person creating the dance or movement elements of a production
Company Manager	the person responsible for managing the company in the theatre
context	the setting of the scene or the emotion of a character
Co-producers	people who share the overall responsibility for presenting the production
creative team	the collective term for the director, choreographer, musical director and others who have artistic responsibilities
cuts	the shortening of music, script or routine
CV	also called Résumé; the details of your career and skills and other valuable information
Dance Captain	the person responsible for maintaining the dance or movement of the production
dance cuts	following a dance call, some will be asked to leave. This is known as being 'cut'
diction	the delivery of words or lyrics
Director	the person responsible for the overall artistic vision and staging of the production
dynamics	the louds and softs of music or speech
ensemble	those members of the company with minimal solo work, also known as chorus
feedback	a response to your audition intended to be useful for the future

General Manager	the person responsible for the day-to-day management of the production
headshot	your professional photograph
intonation	the pitch of the voice
Lead Producer	the senior person with overall responsibility for the production
libretto	the full script
lyrics	the words of a song
Musical Director	the personal responsible for the musical elements of a musical, who may also conduct. There may also be a music supervisor, who is often senior to the musical director
networking	the art of building and maintaining business relationships
panel	the collective term for those judging an audition
props	physical objects to aid the scene
proscenium	the 'framing' at the front of a stage
reader	a non-auditioning member of the team who reads other characters in your scene-work at an audition
recalls	*see* call-backs
repertoire	a collection of songs
résumé	*see* CV
role	a character within a production
score	the music of a musical, also known as the vocal score
script	the text of a musical, or *see* libretto
showcase	a presentation of music, dance or drama, usually by student actors

sides	the scenes of an audition given to auditionees
sight-reading	also known as cold reading, being given text or music in the audition room and asked to perform it immediately without preparation
staccato	quick musical notes
straight theatre	theatrical productions without excessive song or dance
submissions	the presentation of potential actors who are appropriate for the available roles, as defined by the breakdown
swings	actors engaged to understudy the ensemble of a musical. A swing may not necessarily have a regular role in the show, but may understudy several ensemble roles or 'tracks'
tempo	the speed of music, script or dance
tone	a sound with distinct qualities
understudy	an actor who learns the role of another actor in order to be able to act as a replacement if necessary
up-tempo	a quick and often happy song
vocal range	the series of notes a singer can reach, from lowest to highest
warm-up	an exercise, either vocal, physical or physiological, in preparation for the main event, be it singing, dancing or acting audition, or performance

INDEX